Simple Steps to

An

EXTRAORDINARY

Career & Life

Brad Worthley

www.BradWorthley.com

ISBN 978-0-9770668-2-7

Simple Steps to an Extraordinary Career & Life

The content of this book is also available as a seminar. To contact the
author for more information about the seminar, interviews, speaking
engagements, books, DVDs or audio programs:
Brad Worthley International
12819 SE 38th St. #375
Bellevue, WA 98006
(425)957-9696

Please visit our Web site at www.BradWorthley.com

Book layout and design by Stephanie Martindale
Cover design and graphics by Mathes Design
Printed in the United States of America

To my parents, **Harold & Betty Worthley**, who provided a safe and supportive childhood for me to spread my wings and experiment with life. Thank you for supporting me throughout my journey with my many personal and business adventures and for being there during the good times and the bad.

To my friend, **Bill Hyndman**, who taught me about living, as he was dying. It was through his pain that I discovered that life is not a practice round, and we must live each day as if it is our last. It was in his passing that I was given a new mission, to have an extraordinary career and life, and achieve my greatest desires.

To the love of my life, **Melanie**, who has been my partner in living an extraordinary life and supportive in helping me achieve my greatest desires. She is truly one of the most amazing people I have ever met in my life. Melanie is loved and adored by everyone that knows her, both in personal life and at work.

CONTENTS

ACKNOWLEDGEMENTS

To the people who helped get this book completed, with their talents and kindness, including Melanie Compton, Betty Compton, Serin Compton, Kathy Compton, Amy Moretti, Dawn Piasecki, Jordan Lucia, Judy Gay, Barbara Neuhauser and the final eye of Lisa Cosmillo. I am also extremely grateful to my long time graphic artist, Kathy Mathes (www.mathesdesign.com), who designed the book cover and Stephanie Martindale who performed the layout and design of the book.

And to the thousands of newsletter subscribers, facebook friends and Twitter followers from all over the world that were kind enough to offer their valuable time to answer my surveys when I was naming the book. The lessons learned from their feedback was immeasurable and appreciated. Thank you!

INTRODUCTION

I was born rich, but not the way most people would define "rich." I had a wealth of happiness as a child because I was from a small town on the coast of Washington State named Hoquiam, where my recollection of growing up is rich with fond memories. I had known most of the people I went to school with since early grade school, so friends were abundant. I had friends from all social circles, from jocks to what we called "hoods," and I don't remember having any enemies. I struggled with my grades in school, but my grades did not dampen my joy of school and the social networking that I enjoyed so much. I was involved with all sports until I was about 13years old, when I chose to give up sports in order to work at a donut shop so I could earn money for a car when I turned 16.

I was also fortunate because I had incredibly supportive parents who would do anything for me. My father came from a large farming family, which had very little money, so he was raised in tough times. He was happy just to have shoes to wear to school and food on the table for everyone. He worked and retired from a paper mill in Hoquiam, but in an effort to provide my sister and me with the things that he never had as a child, he also worked as a gillnet fisherman for many years. He has always worked very hard, and even in retirement, he maintains tremendous discipline by working out at a gym seven days a week. I learned so much from my father about how to treat people and about working hard for the things you want in life.

My mother was raised in a town even smaller than Hoquiam called Humptulips, which is about 20 miles north of Hoquiam and had a population of only a few hundred people. My mother worked for the phone company for years before she had kids, so when you see old pictures of the early day operators pushing and pulling wires from hole to hole - that was her. After my sister and I were born, she became a stay-at-home mom and was there to make our lunches, see us off to school and be there for us when we got home. Once we were a little bit older, she went to work at Sears, where she worked until her retirement. She was the consummate mother who would do anything for her kids and kept a perfect house along with all the other chores of a home.

My sister Judy and I got along great as kids, and we still do. The biggest fight we might have had was over who was going to sit in the favorite chair or about which television show we were going to watch, so there was very little drama in the house. She was raised the same as I was: with a good work ethic and a lack of empathy for those choosing to play the victim role instead of choosing to work hard. She and her husband are self employed and still work harder than most people would ever want. We still love each other very much today and have tremendous respect for one another.

Maybe time dulls memories, but you would be hard pressed to find much childhood trauma in my life. My early years were like the show *Leave It to Beaver,* and I feel fortunate to have been raised in that environment because I am very aware that not everyone was as lucky. You can see that even though my heritage was not from wealth, I was rich beyond most people's dreams – in simple happiness. With that said, I will tell you that my youth created an internal script within me about who I painted myself to be. The belief I created about myself was that I was from a small town and not as worthy as people from the big cities. I also let my poor grades become who I was, which was "not good enough," and you will see throughout this book how these internal thoughts and feelings about ourselves – regardless of whether they are true or not – shape our destiny if we allow it.

My hope is that this book will open your eyes to the fictitious stories that we create about ourselves, which, for the most part, have no truth behind them. They are simply stories that we have developed loyalty to and have held on to for so many of the wrong reasons. For some people, the stories have been an excuse to stay who we are and to not grow to who we have the ability to become. These stories have allowed many people to play the victim role, which is easy because it requires no action on their part. When I finally became aware of my inner saboteur and the lies behind it, I was able to free myself from its grip and begin the journey to live the extraordinary life that I live today. I have learned that living an extraordinary life and achieving your greatest desires is not a result of your I.Q., your grade point, the amount of money you have today or how lucky you are; it comes from what you believe about yourself.

This book will provide you with the steps that I used to create an extraordinary career and life for myself and my family. The book is not only about having an extraordinary career and life, but achieving your greatest desires, whatever they are for you. For me, it was not just about material things, even though, through the steps in this book, I have been able to provide my family with a summer home, competition ski boat, dream home, investment property, high end cars, fabulous vacations and even a yacht. However, as you will read in this book, I have been able to create an extraordinary life full of love, passion, adventure, great friends, experiences, memories and many other things that cost nothing, but pay huge dividends in the quality of our lives. You can have all of this too, even if deep inside, your brain may not believe it.

An extraordinary life looks different to each of us, so there is no template for evaluating "extraordinary." However, having a well balanced life is important to the process, so before you continue reading this book, I would encourage you to evaluate your current life in order to narrow down what areas might need the most attention. Then, re-score yourself every six months in order to see your progress. Evaluate yourself in each of the following 12 areas of life on a scale of 1 (being poor) and 10 (extraordinary) as to how each one fits into your life. In other words, if you have to work 80 hours a week, you might score "Business & Professional" a 1 or 2. If you are madly in love and your relationship is fabulous with your significant other, you might score yourself a 10. If you do not have children, simply score N/A. If one area of your life is broken, such as relationships, it can negatively impact other areas of your life as well. It is important to address the low scoring areas of life to get you on track to the extraordinary life you deserve.

AREAS OF LIFE	TODAY	6 MOS	1 YR
Business & Professional			
Personal Finance (Savings & retirement acct)			
Relationship with Significant Other			
Relationship with Your Children			
Relationship with Other Family			
Friendships			
Hobbies and Recreation			
Physical Health (Weight, medical, physically fit)			
Emotional Health (Stress, confidence, attitude)			
Intellectual Health (Learning & development)			
Spiritually (Religion, meditation, etc.)			
Social & Service (Serving others)			

Before you begin, I would like to offer you a suggestion about some of the self-talk that you will encounter and how it might impede your opportunity for learning. As you are reading this book, if your brain starts saying "*I know that*" about its content, ask yourself the question, "*Do I do that?*" What you know is not as important as what you do. So many people possess the knowledge to live an extraordinary life and achieve their greatest desires but fail to take the actions necessary to make it become a reality. Are you one of those voracious readers of self-help books who do nothing with your knowledge? My encouragement to you is to break free from the emotional shackles that bind you and take the first step towards change.

Chapter 1
CLARIFYING YOUR DESIRES

The definition of "desire" is to want strongly or to crave. Everyone has desires, but they certainly vary depending on your current economic situation and your environment. For people who have very little, their desire might be for simple things such as food, shelter, a vehicle or even a job. Their desire may be as generic as simply wanting more from life and an urgency to leave behind their current life for a more fulfilling one. It might be wrapped around the selfless desire to want more for their family and children, or it may be selfishly wanting to take care of their own needs and cravings even at the expense of others.

For the middle class, it may be a nicer car, family boat, bigger home, a promotion, dream vacation, wanting children or many other material things that might bring perceived joy. Where people of lesser means might define some of their desires as "needs", the middle class might be more inclined to define many of their desires as "wants". The problem with having stuff is that there is always stuff that you don't have, and if you are laying awake watching television at two o'clock in the morning, you are going to see stuff that you can't live without. They have stuff on television at that hour that you did not even know you needed until they convinced you that your life would be better with it, and since you are only half awake at that hour, you actually agree with them and buy it (*"But wait, there's more! Buy now, and we will double your order!"*).

People of greater wealth also have desires, and they have the means to make their desires become a reality. If they desire a yacht, they will buy it. If they want a winter home in Sun Valley, then they will simply fulfill their desire and buy it. This group also falls under the "want" and not necessarily "need" category. Many people in this financial segment of the population fulfill their desires in an attempt to bring them happiness or gratification. As most of us know, this is simply a carrot that is dangled in front of us trying to convince us that once we reach the carrot, life will be better. Once we consume the carrot, then we will need another carrot to fulfill our

The problem with having stuff is that there is always stuff that you don't have

endless appetite for wanting to be happy and believing that "things" will achieve that. Our desires become never ending and happiness is always about "someday," which is like the eighth day of the week that never comes. The problem is that people who are waiting for "someday" or tomorrow to be happy do not enjoy life today because they are sitting at the front door and waiting for happiness to arrive (it is always in the future). People who live like this are continually disappointed and prone to depression.

For the more spiritual or less materialistic people, their desires may be for a higher education, being stress-free, world peace, eliminating famine from the earth, good health of family and friends or other non-material requests. It might be the desire to help others or to serve the community as a whole, and thank goodness the world has many of these selfless people. As many people have thankfully learned, the giver's rewards can be far greater than the receiver's. What I mean by that is the act of giving to others is selfish in some ways because the feelings of gratification that come with philanthropy are so huge that givers sometimes get more out of the process than the receivers.

There are also people caught up in circumstances which they may not be able to control that can create very focused desires regardless of their economic situation or spiritual beliefs. If you are having a baby, your desire might be focused on nothing more than for a healthy baby. The world around you and your personal economics are background noise to the joy of having a healthy baby. If you have been diagnosed with cancer, your desires become focused on survival, so wealth or material things mean very little to you at this point. Your desires take on a new meaning if you are struggling for your life because success can come in the form of a CT scan that shows no tumor, blood tests showing signs of improvement or an encouraging smile on the doctor's face.

People's desires are personal and difficult to judge because we have not walked in each other's shoes. I think everyone should have desires, which if transformed into specific goals and timelines, can be very motivating and productive. They can give us a reason to wake up every day and give us hope about the future. Everyone wants better for themselves, but the word "better" is subjective and takes on different meanings for each of us, and that is the great thing about desires.

Regardless of social or economic class, there are also desires we have that have nothing to do with "want" and everything to do with "need." In other words, our desires may have found us, and it is our mission to make these desires become a reality, or they could cost us not only our health, but our lives. As an example, if you are 5' 5" and 300 pounds with high blood pressure, high cholesterol, and a history of family members dying young from heart disease, it may become one of your greatest desires to lose weight. This is not an option, this is not a "want," it is an urgent "need" with the penalty for failure so severe that you are motivated to make your desire become a reality.

You are 42 years old, been smoking most of your life and may have tried many times to stop but just could not seem to find the discipline. You watched your remaining parent die a slow and painful death at 60 years old from lung cancer because they were also lifetime smokers. You are now painfully aware that based on family history, you will more than likely only have 18 more summers with your friends at the summer cabin, 18 more Christmases with your family, 18 more birthdays and 18 more Valentine's Days with which to celebrate the love for your significant other. If that thought would not motivate you to have the desire to stop smoking, nothing will.

You are the life of the party and everyone wants to be around you because you are fun. You live to party and party as you live. You enjoy a good cocktail and find enjoyment having a couple for lunch and a few in the evening just to wind down at the end of a hard day. At your annual physical, your blood results showed your liver is deteriorating from the alcohol abuse. The doctor warns you that if you continue this lifestyle, you will destroy your liver and more than likely be dead within the next couple of years. Your new desire might be one of sobriety in order to allow you to enjoy a healthy life, because the consequence of not stopping could be death.

Whatever your desires may be, this book will provide the process for looking at many areas of your life and helping you achieve your desires. There is no magic pill or shortcut to the process, so it still requires work on your part, but the work gets easier as you understand more about yourself. I believe that awareness can help bring change, so my goal is to create awareness of the things that keep us stuck in the place we are today, so we can move forward and get to where we choose to be. The end result is, for you to have an extraordinary career and life, and achieve your greatest desires.

Chapter 2
THE THREE LEVELS OF DESIRE

When I ask people in my seminars what their desires are, they run the full spectrum of the basics to the extreme. Below are examples of what I have heard:

For Business:

- *Write a book*
- *Buy into a franchise*
- *Become a consultant*
- *Invent a new product*
- *Get an idea patented*
- *Make $250,000 a year*
- *Take leadership classes*
- *Start their own business*
- *Be on a Board of Directors*
- *Become a branch manager*
- *Become certified as a coach*
- *Become CEO of a company*

- *Become a partner in our firm*
- *Learn to be a professional speaker*
- *Become manager of their department*

For Personal:

- *Race cars*
- *Lose weight*
- *Take up golf*
- *Quit smoking*
- *Run a marathon*
- *Work in a winery*
- *Buy a fishing boat*
- *Be happily married*
- *Go to a Super Bowl*
- *Climb Mount Rainier*
- *Get a Master's Degree*
- *Compete in a Triathlon*
- *Build their dream home*
- *Retire when they are 50*
- *Build their own sailboat*
- *Ride a bike across the U.S.*
- *Visit every country in the world*
- *Pay for their grandchildren's college*

As you can see, people's desires come in all shapes and sizes. Why is it that some of these people will achieve their desires and others will not? Will it have to do with their I.Q., what their grade point was in school, the amount of money their family has, the people that they know, expertise around their desire, or the amount of hours devoted to achieving their desire? Some of these things may help people achieve their desires and might provide an easier path to success, but one of the real keys is the level of importance that each person attaches to their desires.

We can categorize desire into three levels of importance:

Three Levels of Desire:

1. *Important*
2. *Very important*
3. ***Most* *important***

As an example, many people might believe that it is "Important" to stop smoking. Some might even know that it is "Very important" to them; but when it becomes "Most important" to them, the chances of achieving their goal increase dramatically. The word "Most" applies when you are passionate about your desire, and it takes precedence over other priorities in your life. This is the point where you are motivated and discipline will kick in to make your desires more attainable.

Take the example I gave in the last chapter about the smoker who watched their parent die of lung cancer. My guess would be that they knew it was "Important" to stop smoking at some point, and they may have even reached the point where they knew it was "Very Important." However, stopping smoking may have just become the "Most Important" thing to them when they lost their last parent, and they are now fully committed to stopping when they began to realize the imminence of their own mortality.

I honestly believe that when many people use the words "Important" or "Very important" that they might truly believe it, but they are not necessarily motivated to action. My personal belief is that within these two levels of desire lies apathy for many people. The dictionary defines apathy as the lack of interest, enthusiasm or energy to do something, which simply means that some people may have desires but not the motivation to move them to reality. There might be many reasons why people are not willing to fully commit to their desires, but one of the biggest reasons why people will thwart their efforts is fear, which we will cover in tremendous detail as you move through this book.

As a personal example of the levels of desire, I will tell you that I love great food and fine wine. When I pick up a menu in a restaurant, I am tortured by the number of items on the menu that I want to try because I like most everything. When the server asks me what I want, my first thought is to tell them I want page one and to keep it coming until I explode. So, it is really easy for me to pack on unwanted weight, and trust me, it is all unwanted.

The reason I mention my eating habits is because diabetes runs very strongly on my mother's side of the family. Her father had it, both of her sisters got it, and most of their children got it. It seems that most were introduced to it around the age of 60, and the trigger seemed to be when they put on excess weight. My mother is the only one not to get it, but she has always been skinny as a rail and works hard to keep her weight under control. She has walked three to five miles-a-day for the last 20 or more years, so her health has been important to her. Diabetes created many related health issues in our family such as vision loss, having legs amputated, dementia, Alzheimer's and other symptomatic problems.

My fear is that if I do not keep my weight under control, I will end up with diabetes because diabetes can be linked to heredity. I do not enjoy working out, and I do not enjoy early mornings, however keeping my weight under control is the "Most important" thing to me. There is nothing that has a higher priority in my life because if I end up with the disease it may impede the quality of my life and all the things I enjoy may no longer be possible. I get up at 5 a.m. five days a week and go to the gym to work out – not because I like to, but because I choose to in order to keep my weight down and reduce the chances of getting diabetes.

Even though we all know weight loss is "Important" and most of us even know it is "Very important", one-third of American adults are obese because they do not think it is "Most important" to them I consider myself very proactive, and I am good at both trying to anticipate my pain and working to prevent it. Unfortunately, most people are reactive and live their lives without thought of the future. Most people will say to themselves that "someday" they will lose the weight (someday is like the 8th day of the week that never comes). Then, when it is too late, and diabetes, heart disease or other illnesses take them over, the reactive drill begins of how to deal with it, which can be too late for many.

Writing this book is another example of the level of desires and what it takes to be motivated enough to drive our desires to action. I have wanted to write this book for more than a year because it was "Important" to my business. However, I had other priorities such as updating my Web site, building new seminars and many other projects that had more immediate importance. After about six months, I came to the realization that I had been putting off writing this book because I don't necessarily enjoy the writing process (as compared to other tasks that I have), so at a subconscious level, many other things seemed more important (especially the pleasurable ones). Once I developed clarity around that, I moved the book up on my mental list to make it "Very important," so it finally made it to the to-do list on my desk. I stared at my list each day and knew the book needed to be done soon because I wanted to go to print in six months.

someday is like the 8th day of the week that never comes

About this same time, I began performing the seminar for my clients and the response was overwhelming. I was getting feedback from attendees like "*This is life changing!*" or "*I learned more in four hours than I did in six months of therapy*" and the seminar evaluation scores from the attendees were the highest I have ever had in my 20 years (such as 9.7 out of a total 10, which is near perfect). I realized

I needed to get this book written soon in order to support the seminars and give people a take-away because this seminar was taking off quickly. I decided that the book was now the "Most important" thing I had to do, so I scheduled time each morning to write. I scheduled myself from 7:30 to 8:30 a.m. each day and rarely faltered on my schedule. If my morning got thwarted for some reason, I would make up for it by working late to get caught up. The book became a reality when I made the choice to make it the "Most important" thing to me.

What is on your list of things to do and what level of importance do you give each of them? What items are ignored and how "Important" are those items to you in the great scheme of things? Are they simply tasks or is one of them a "desire" that you have ignored? If it is truly a "desire" (something you want strongly or crave), then what would it take to make it "Most important" and motivate you to action? If it is not that "Important" to you, then that is certainly OK. I am just asking you to be realistic about the things you call "desires" and give them the due amount of importance so you can prioritize your energy and make the "Most important" ones become reality. The only thing that may be standing between you, an extraordinary career and life, and your greatest desires is you!

Chapter 3

THE MOTIVATORS

In the last chapter, we talked about motivation being one of the requirements to achieving your desires by driving you to action. Is it possible that some of you will never attain your desires because you are stuck in the "Very important" level of desire and not motivated enough to move it to "Most important"? Once you find the motivation to move it to "Most important," you are now committing yourself to action and a higher level of accountability. For many people, that is going to be uncomfortable and might be the thing that drives you back to the "Very important" level, which is safe because it requires no action on your part.

In 2007, there was a movie produced titled *The Bucket List* (starring Morgan Freeman and Jack Nicholson) about a couple of guys who were terminally ill and made a list of all the things they wanted to do before they died. It is a great movie about living life to its fullest and in the process, doing a lot of self-discovery. These two guys were motivated by their impending deaths to achieve some of their greatest desires. Wouldn't it be great if we were motivated to achieve our greatest desires and seek to live an extraordinary life without a motivator that is as definitive as death?

A friend of mine whom I had known since grade school, Bill Hyndman, lived with his family in Eastern Washington in a small development on the Columbia River named Desert Aire. I stopped by to visit him one sunny, hot July day and discovered a fabulous community with a golf course and the calmest water you have ever seen. Being a golfer and avid water skier, I fell in love that weekend with this area, bought a piece of property and built a summer home to enjoy with my family.

I had the pleasure of watching Bill at play with his two sons and daughter as they grew up. He was the kind of dad I wanted to be. He bought a house with a swimming pool for the kids, he took them boating and taught them how to ski and golf. Both he and his wife Kelsey were very active in the community, and they seemed to have a great life.

I can remember vividly when Bill and I were 40 years old and golfing together one gorgeous, sunny 80 degree day at Desert Aire. He told me that his house was almost paid off, his children's college fund was in place, he was investing in property, and at this rate, he was planning to retire at the age of 45. His job took him away from home sometimes for months at a time, but, he said, the sacrifice was worth it. He told me that once he retires, his kids would still be in school, and he could have all the time on earth to go to their sporting events and maybe even help coach their teams.

I was envious of Bill, because even though I had been successful in my own businesses, I was nowhere near being able to retire. Four years later, Bill told me that he had found some swelling in his lymph nodes, and the doctors diagnosed it as cancer. They began treatments for his disease, which were draining him of his energy and making it difficult for him to work. Bill stopped working at the age of 45, but it was not the retirement he had so methodically planned – it was a medical leave from his job.

About a year after that, I was playing golf at my summer home in Desert Aire with my son, Tate, on another fabulous sunny, dry day. The mountain across the river loomed large, the river was so calm it was like a mirror, and the smell of sage filled the air. I developed tremendous guilt that I was enjoying a magnificent day with my son, while I knew Bill was in the hospital fighting for his life. It all of a sudden hit me that I could have easily been the one in Bill's shoes – why him and not me? I also realized that it could easily be me tomorrow or the next day. As I stood in the middle of the golf course pondering my questions, I realized for the first time that life is not a practice round.

I knew I could no longer take each day for granted and that I needed to be thankful for just being healthy. I committed myself on that day to taking more time to smell the roses and to telling those around me how much they mean to me. When I got home, I E-mailed Bill, who was at the Fred Hutchinson Cancer Research Center in Seattle. I told him of my revelation and thanked him for giving me a renewed outlook on life. I told him that no other person in my life has had so much impact, given the fact that his suffering breathed new life into me and gave me a greater appreciation for each day.

I realized for the first time that life is not a practice round

Less than a week later, at the age of 46, Bill passed away. After I spoke at his funeral, a woman approached me and introduced herself as the person who was taking care of Bill in his final days. She told me that Bill had not only been suffering from cancer but also with the question as to how his death would serve the world. Bill was very committed to God and his church, but he was perplexed with who could possibly benefit from his pain and eventual demise. He could not understand God's plan and it frustrated him.

She told me that on the day I sent the E-mail, Bill was too weak to even get out of bed, so she read my E-mail to him. After she finished reading it to him, she turned around and saw Bill ease back into his pillow with the first look of tranquility she had seen in months. She asked if he was OK, and he said, "*Yes, I am very well.*" He told her that he finally got the answer to his nagging question. Bill had figured out that it was me who he had touched and dramatically changed forever. He passed away peacefully a few days later knowing that his death was not in vain.

It was at that moment that I began creating a list of all the things that I wanted to do before I died. This was ten years before *The Bucket List* ever came out, so I was ahead of my time, but I swore I was going to achieve as many of the things on my list as I could and commit to living an extraordinary life. Here are some of the things on my list:

- *Super Bowl*
- *Own a yacht*
- *Visit Europe*
- *Write a Book*
- *Grand Canyon*
- *NASCAR race*
- *Visit Australia*
- *Broadway play*
- *Build dream home*
- *Ride in a private jet*
- *White water rafting*
- *Napa Valley wine tasting*
- *Own investment property*
- *Have a three-week vacation*
- *Mardi Gras in New Orleans*
- *Seventh game of a World Series*
- *Sonoma Valley wine tasting*
- *Times Square for New Year's*
- *Own a convertible sports car*

- *Community volunteer work*
- *Monster truck national finals*
- *Visit wine country in Europe*

Over the last ten years, I have achieved everything on the list above and about 80 percent of all the things on my complete list, but I keep adding to it as well, so it may never be finalized. Bill's passing was a huge motivator for me to be more intentional about what I want out of life, take risks and appreciate each and every day. The pain of Bill's passing became a motivator for me to change my life. I am thankful for that gift and hope it truly did give Bill's passing some meaning.

Motivation comes to people in many ways, sometimes based on circumstances or events, but there are two primary motivators that impact our decision making every day throughout our lives. These two motivators inspire us to change, or at the least, alter our perceptions of people, events and circumstances.

There are two things that will motivate people to change:

1. *Pain*

2. *Pleasure*

I am not sure whether one motivator is more powerful than the other because it is based on each person's experience and the circumstance that creates either the pain or the pleasure. For me, it was the pain of losing a friend that motivated me to an awakening about how precious life is and that I shall be grateful for each day. Bill's passing touched hundreds of people who knew him, but was anyone else motivated to change their thoughts, feelings or actions as well? I shall never know, but I sure hope so.

Change is hard for humans, so we will resist change. Change requires action, so it is far easier to not change. One of the reasons we resist change is simply the fear of the unknown. Not knowing the path we may have to take in our change, or worse yet, not knowing the outcome and how it might impact us is scary. Humans will find almost any reason to avoid risk; often times by creating stories in their head that aren't even true. I don't think there is a better salesperson than a person challenged by the question as to whether they should change or not. They will work very hard at selling themselves out of the idea, and most will succeed. The interesting thing is, if we lack answers to our questions or if we are void of information, most people tend to fill the void with negative information (a negative story). This is one of the reasons why so many people will never achieve their desires: it's not for the lack of talent or resources, but the stories they create in their head that keep them from taking action.

When it comes to achieving your desires, taking action becomes more probable as the rate of perceived pain or pleasure increases. The more you feel the pain, the greater level of importance you will attach to your desire. The same is true for pleasure, because the more pleasure you anticipate, the greater level of importance you will attach to your desire. See the following chart and how as both the perceived pain and pleasure increase (whether it is real or not is unimportant), so does the level of desire:

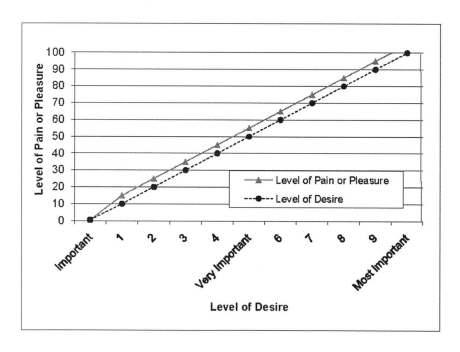

In mid-October of 2006, the love of my life, Melanie, got out of the bathtub and mentioned her skin itched badly and it would not stop. We assumed that it might have been the bath oil that she used, so we dismissed it as a topical issue (as something on top of the skin that created the itch, like the bath oil). The itching did not stop, and it progressively got worse, so we considered all the possibilities and changed laundry detergent, soap and anything else that we believed could be causing this unusual condition. We even rewashed all of her clothes in allergy free washing soap, which we believed would eliminate the itching, but it did not.

Each day it got worse. By the second week, she was scratching herself so hard that she was bruising and damaging her skin. One day, her mother stopped by her office and chatted with her briefly and asked if she was feeling alright because she did not look normal. When her mom got home, she called back to Melanie and asked if her urine was dark yellow and Melanie confirmed that it was. Her mother, who did medical transcription for many years, told Melanie that she believed she might have Hepatitis because of the color of her urine and the fact that Melanie's eyes were also yellowed. She encouraged her to get to the doctor right away and get checked out, which we did.

We arrived at her primary care physician's office, and they took blood samples and sent them off to the lab. The next day, we were sent to the emergency room where they performed an ultra sound on her around the mid section of her torso. They gave us a prescription for a drug to help reduce her itching then sent us home for the night. The next day, they called and requested us to come back to the hospital where they requested a CT scan to get a better look at her internal organs. We were waiting in the emergency room for some type of word on what her condition might be, fearing what we thought would be the worst case scenario, which would have been Hepatitis. A couple of hours later, the emergency room doctor came into the room holding his cell phone and told Melanie that they had her primary doctor on the telephone, who wanted to talk to her. Melanie picked up the telephone, listened intently for a couple of minutes and then a look came over her face that I will never forget because her face went blank and almost numb from shock. Her doctor informed her that she had pancreatic cancer.

They requested that we go home, go on-line and read about pancreatic cancer while they put a plan in place to find solutions. We walked out of the hospital in complete disbelief and utter shock. How could she have cancer? She has no cancer in her family, and pancreatic cancer normally impacts people in their 70s, not someone who is a healthy 51 years young. Thank goodness, the drugs they gave her hit hard, and when she got home, she immediately fell asleep. The news of that day changed not only Melanie's life, but the lives of everyone who knew her.

Melanie is one of the most amazing people I have ever had the pleasure to know, and you will be hard-pressed to ever find anyone as fabulous. Everyone loves this woman, and she makes friends with everyone she comes into contact with. My love for her is immeasurable, and there is nothing I would not do for her. She has three wonderful kids (from a previous marriage) who love and adore her and an entire family that is rich in love and kindness. Melanie and her entire family have enriched my life beyond my wildest dreams, and it was absolutely terrifying to know that she had a disease that wanted to kill her.

I began to read about pancreatic cancer on-line, and there was absolutely no good news to be found. Most Web sites said the same thing: Approximately 4 percent of the people diagnosed with pancreatic cancer will survive five years, but most will not make it even one year. My heart raced, and my body heated up as a flash of my life without this incredible woman passed before me, and I became terrified. At that moment, her survival became the "Most important" thing in my life. If you look back a few pages, there is a diagram depicting how as the perceived level of pain goes up, so does the level of importance; well my perceived pain was off the top of the chart. If there was a level beyond "Most important," I was there and the motivators kicked in full blast.

We notified the entire family and our close friends about the new journey we were now on, and they rallied around us and came to our rescue. They cooked and cleaned for us while I was busy doing my research, plus kept Melanie occupied with games, movies, and anything else to keep her mind off her diagnosis. My own family reminded me that we'd had a few of our own battles with pancreatic cancer over the years. It had taken the lives of both of my grandmothers as well as that of an uncle. This was a fact that I had completely forgotten. What I did remember was how painful their deaths were and how quickly they passed away after they were diagnosed. Here I was the one with a family history of this dreadful disease, yet Melanie was the one to get it, not me.

The drugs they gave her were fabulous because even though she looked like she was functioning normally, they helped eliminate the anxiety of each day and kept her disenfranchised from reality. From morning to night, my days were filled with on-line research trying to find the experts in this field who could save her life. I called every hospital in the United States that had experts on this type of cancer, and most of them referred me back to the Northwest, where we had some local experts. The doctor that kept popping up as the person with the most experience in the type of surgery she needed, called a "Whipple Procedure," was at the University Medical Center in Seattle, which was only a 15- minute drive. Being proactive, I also got the names of two other doctors in two other hospitals who were also very good, just as a backup.

The doctor at our local hospital, where our diagnosis was first given, told us that he would be able to get us an appointment with a surgeon in about four weeks to review our case and schedule surgery for a later date. I knew pancreatic cancer well enough by now to know that time is not on our side, so I began to call the three doctors that I had researched as our best options. Each of the doctor's offices told me that they were very busy, and it would be four weeks before we could even get a first introduction appointment. I begged for quicker action or other alternatives, but to no avail. Meanwhile, our local hospital checked Melanie back in for a surgery to implant a stent into a bile duct to open it up, which would help reduce the itching and buy us some time until she could have the Whipple procedure. The machine that they use to implant the stent broke down for some reason, so they had to stop the procedure about half way through and send her back to her room. We were told that they would have the machine fixed, and the stent operation was rescheduled for the next day.

I made the decision that day that I would not allow her to die, and if 4 percent can survive this horrific cancer, she would be one of the 4 percent (Why not? Someone has to be it). Remembering that saving her life is the "Most important" thing to me, I decided I needed to be willing to take extraordinary measures if I wanted to continue to have my extraordinary life with this fabulous woman. The stent surgery that they were going to do on her tomorrow was not going to fix her; it was just going to buy us time. Furthermore, it still put her at risk because of the potential for complications and possible death (and there was a likelihood of that with this intricate operation).

I took the CD disc of the CT scans that the hospital gave us and burned three copies on my laptop computer. I made a collage of family photos on an 8" x 10" sheet of photo paper, which showed Melanie at play with her family. I know that doctors see CT scans every day, but they do not always get to see the face of the people who they are making decisions about. I knew I had to pull out all the stops, so tugging at a doctor's heart strings was not beyond my abilities. I also grabbed three copies of my first book titled "The Ultimate Guide to Exceeding Customer Expectations" (Did you expect anything less from me at this point?). I put on my favorite (and lucky) purple shirt, suit and tie, packed the CT scan discs, photos of Melanie, and my three autographed books and drove to each doctor's office to drop them off.

My first stop was the University of Washington Medical Center because the doctor who had the most experience with this type of surgery was a gentleman named Dr. Mika Sinanan. His secretary met me and was very nice as she, once again, explained how busy he was, but she would be glad to take him the things I had delivered. After I left the U of W Medical Center, I went to the other hospitals in Seattle and made my delivery to their offices as well, also being told that the chances were slim of an appointment within four weeks, let alone surgery. I was driving back to our local hospital where Melanie was waiting for her stent surgery the next day, and my cell phone rang. I answered and it was Dr. Sinanan himself. He told me that he looked at her information, and if I could bring her into the hospital this afternoon, he would perform the Whipple Procedure, which she so desperately needed tomorrow morning. I drove back to the local hospital, checked her out and drove her immediately to the U of W hospital where we checked her in. The seven-hour surgery was performed successfully on November 4, 2006, and Dr. Sinanan told us that her cancer tumor was pressing against an artery, and it almost wrapped it. If that would have happened, he would not have been able to do the surgery and the outcome could have been much different.

Melanie is indeed on her way to becoming one of the lucky 4 percent that survive more than five years because as of the writing of this book, she is four years along, healthy and cancer free. My question to you is: what are you willing to do, that no one else is willing to do, in order to have the things that no one else has? I did something that most people might not have done in order to save Melanie's life because it was the "Most important" thing to me. It was the "Most important" thing to me because the perceived level of pain was so high. What is the "Most important" thing to you and what are you willing to do in order to achieve it? Which motivator is the driving force behind your desire: pain or pleasure? An extraordinary life requires extraordinary actions, so give serious consideration to your desires and what motivates you.

Pain and pleasure are used in many areas of our lives to shape human behavior. In the world of commerce, people who have a product to sell will try to find some way to instill pain or pleasure into you to motivate you to buy. On the pleasure side, they will tell you how attractive you will become and how pleasurable your life will be if you buy the new Challenger 3000 Nose Hair Removal Kit for only $19.95 – **BUT WAIT,** there's more! You buy the Challenger 3000 in the next 30 minutes and we will throw in the ear hair removal attachment for free. **BUT WAIT,** there's more! Act now and we will double your offer! How could you possibly say no to these products?

Or you will see businesses try to get you to anticipate some perceived amount of pain if you do not purchase their product: If you don't buy the new Dental Lab Diesel Powered Flossing Machine for only $19.95, you may end up with gum disease, which could lead to brain tumors, athlete's foot, poor cuticles, loss of limbs or the pain of hemorrhoid tissue. Well, you can't take a chance on any of those, so of course you will pick up the phone at three o'clock in the morning and order a dozen for everyone in the family in order to save them from this potential pain.

We also use these two methods with our children when we want to move them toward change of some sort. Being the supportive and loving parents that we are, we seek to show our children the benefits (pleasure) of cleaning their room, doing their homework, dumping the garbage, cleaning the cat box, or any other darling of a duty that we don't want to do either. We try to make these tasks pleasurable by offering them allowance, providing them with praise, buying a new video game for them or cooking their favorite meal. For some children, this method works really well, but for others, not so much.

Some children still might not be motivated by these pleasurable offerings that you have tempted them with. Or, these pleasures worked for a while when they were younger, but then they became teenagers and OH MY GOSH! What went wrong with the pleasure train, and why did it come to a screeching halt? Why is it that two weeks ago, when they were 12, these temptations worked perfectly and today at 13, the child seems to have developed an immunity to our generosity? Now, out of frustration, you step over to the dark-side and start looking at the pain alternatives. Your smile has disappeared, your friendly and loving demeanor has gone south, you have now resorted to your best "stink eye" and your tone has turned somewhat Satanic in an effort to motivate your child. You enlighten them to some of the potential pains that could occur if they do not do the things you have asked. You educate them about the pains of being grounded and not being able to see their friends. You dangle the loss of television privileges, no more video games, maybe additional chores, and then you hit them where it hurts the most; they might lose their cell phone (i.e., critical mobile social networking communication device).

We use this exact same methodology with our employees by offering them the many benefits of doing what they are told or achieving specific levels of performance. We offer them incentives such as bonuses, extra time off, non-cash awards like gift cards for a little extra effort, or we dangle promotions in front of their faces. We offer them praise and recognition, which is the top motivator for most people and demonstrate by our actions how valuable they are to the organization. These methods work great with most people because they are pleasurable, and who does not enjoy something pleasurable?

However, all humans are not created equal, and they do not all respond the same to similar motivators. Sometimes you might be motivated, once again, to step over to the dark-side and enlighten them to the potential penalties (pains) if they fail to perform. We need to educate them about the consequences involved in making poor decisions about their performance because decisions are simply opportunities to weigh rewards against consequences and see which one brings the most pain or pleasure. So we let them know that the consequences for failure to perform could be a verbal reprimand, written warning, loss of pay, unpaid time off, or potential loss of job. You simply hope the potential pain is enough to motivate them to action. However, if used too often and in a threatening manner, this method could lead to resentment and resentment can lead to retaliation of some sort. So I would only use the pain motivator as a last means of action.

Pain and pleasure are motivators for us, and you will find ways to utilize these tools in your personal life as well. In 1999, I went through a divorce, and I would have to define it as a very painful experience. That pain, just like the pain I felt with my friend Bill Hyndman (a sense of loss), motivated me to evaluate my life and give consideration to changes that I might not normally make. As I said before, people hate change, and I am no different. Change that I would have normally fought or not even considered became acceptable in the state of pain that I was in.

I evaluated what parts of my life were working and what parts were not. I made a list of the things that stressed me out and drained me of energy (gave me pain), and a separate list of the things that made me happy and gave me energy (brought me pleasure). Most of the things on the energy draining list had to do with the part of my company that performed mystery shopping services (also referred to as secret shopping). For those who might not be familiar with those terms, we used to send people into businesses, and they would go through a normal transaction or interaction with the employees and then report back how they felt about the level of service being provided. We did this for retail stores, banks, fast food restaurants, athletic clubs, car rental companies, grocery stores, spas, casinos, call centers and many other businesses throughout the United States.

Here is an example of my list that helped bring clarity to my life:

Things that drain me of energy (pain)	Things that give me energy (pleasure)
My Employees	*My son*
Mystery Shoppers	*Friends*
Expensive office leases	*Summer home*
Expensive office equipment	*Volunteer work*
Monthly time-lines set by clients	*Public speaking*
Big house which required time	*Consulting & Coaching*

At the time, I had 35 full-time employees, 95,000 mystery shoppers in our database, a large office in a business park, expensive office equipment and all the stuff that goes along with a growing company. It was all the stuff that was draining me of energy. I had great employees, but I was spending most of my time dealing with their issues and not doing enough of the things that gave me energy. It was also very stressful trying to orchestrate and schedule 95,000 independent mystery shoppers. Many were fabulous to work with, but with others, it was like trying to herd cats. It provided me with a good living, but it also provided me with the most stress. The pain of my divorce gave me the opportunity to be introspective and to create clarity about how the mystery shopping part of the business was a drain on me. So, I sold that part of my company to a firm in Houston, Texas shortly after my divorce, and it turned out to be a fabulous decision.

About seven years prior to my divorce, I built my dream home in an exclusive community in Bellevue, Washington, with a gorgeous unobstructed view of Mount Rainer. It had electric blinds, a media room, a wine cellar, marble floors, granite counter tops and the furniture was custom made for the home. Building my dream home had been one of my desires, and one I achieved before the age of 40. However, the amount of work involved in maintaining the home was exhausting and left less time for the things I love to do (things on my "give me energy list"). I spent at least three days a week working on the yard or around the house. I realized the home, even though it was my dream home, was a drain on my energy and diverted me away from the things that were really important in my life, so I sold it – no regrets!

I began to focus on the things that gave me energy. On the top of the list was my son, so being a coach and helping with his sports became a higher priority. Spending more time with the friends who are supportive of me and give me energy was also important, so I committed to more time with them. My summer home was also a great place to help me recharge my battery and give me energy, so I created more time to spend over there. I also found time for volunteer work, even though it took a couple of years to make it become a reality. The consulting and speaking part of my business was what really got me excited to get up each day, so I wanted to focus more on that. I became motivated to re-define and re-invent my firm into the organization that it is today, Brad Worthley International (www.BradWorthley. com), which is exactly what serves me best. I can honestly say that I live an extraordinary life today because I found the motivation to make dramatic and intentional changes in my life because of the two motivators: pain and pleasure.

> *I began to focus on the things that gave me energy*

We have talked about pain and pleasure as motivators; now let's break them down a little further in order to better understand each. First, let's break down pain a little bit because there are two types of pain motivators.

Within the realm of pain as a motivator, there are two forms:

1. *Physical Pain*

2. *Emotional Pain*

Physical pain is pretty easy to understand because in order to avoid being hurt, we might change our behavior. In other words if you were at a party and someone much larger than you bumped into you and made you mad, based on their size and the entourage of friends, you might be motivated to walk away such as to avoid a potentially painful beating. If you were cooking and you had to remove a hot pan from the oven, you might be motivated to use an oven-mitt in order to avoid the pain of a serious burn.

I mentioned earlier in the book how diabetes was a motivator for me to get up at five in the morning and go to the gym in order to keep my weight down. This is also a good example of how the potential for pain motivates me to action. This might be the same motivator that could get someone to stop taking illegal drugs, to quit smoking, to stop drinking and driving, or simply get a physical examination or mammogram to reduce the worry of what potential ailment is going undetected. The threat of physical pain is a motivator for most people to change their behavior, redirect their actions or, at the very least, give tremendous consideration to their thoughts before they become action.

Now, let's take a deeper look into emotional pain as a motivator and how it might move us to action.

Emotional Pain
- *Fear*
- *Guilt*
- *Failure*
- *Rejection*
- *Humiliation*
- *Embarrassment*

Fear is one of the primary motivators because it can quickly drive us to action by its immediate perceived threat. Fear is not necessarily reality, it is the anticipation of something that may or may not exist. That anticipation can motivate us to action because we might choose to avoid the perceived pain. In other words, a child might be motivated by fear to be home at a specific time as requested by their parents in order to avoid the pain of being disciplined. Fear might motivate an employee to work extra hard to get a project completed on time in order to avoid the feelings of disappointment or a reprimand.

Guilt can also motivate us to change. For example, an employee might be motivated to increase their productivity at work in order to keep up with their coworkers and not feel guilty about their lower performance. A husband might be motivated to thwart off the advances of another woman due to the feelings of guilt he might be subjected to if he steps over the line. You might be motivated to be more proactive and leave early for a dinner engagement, so you can avoid the guilt from arriving late and having people waiting impatiently for you, which might make you feel guilty.

Failure has to be on the top of the list when it comes to motivators because most of us fear failure. We could be philosophical and say that there is no such thing as failure, only lessons learned, but as great as that sounds, it is still emotionally traumatizing for most people to fail. There are many daily examples of how the fear of failure will motivate us as children, parents, employees or leaders. As children, we might be motivated to study harder and pay more attention in class in order not to fail an assignment or end up with failing grades. We are sometimes motivated to become active in our children's activities such as school or sports, even though our schedule may not easily allow it, because we do not want to fail as parents. Many employees are motivated to listen to their supervisor, follow instructions and go about their job with due diligence because they do not want to fail at their duties. As leaders, we might be motivated to be a great example for the people we serve and avoid behaviors that might tarnish our role, so we do not fail as leaders.

Rejection can certainly be a motivator to most people and especially to children who are in school. Acceptance is something that most kids strive for, and when not achieved, it can become an emotional wound that lasts a lifetime. The motivator here is to avoid rejection, so we might alter our behaviors or dress in order to fit in with a particular crowd. Even as adults, we still continue to seek acceptance by our peers, so we avoid behaviors that might isolate us. Unfortunately, in order to fit in, some people become chameleons and give up who they are to seek acceptance at the expense of their own authenticity. This can lead to attracting people into your life that are wrong for you.

Humiliation can prove to be a motivator for almost anyone because no one wants to be or feel humiliated (which can be defined as a loss of dignity or pride). Some people might be motivated to drink in moderation at parties or company events because they would not want to become intoxicated and behave in a way that might humiliate themselves. An actor might be motivated to study their lines relentlessly, so they don't get on stage, forget their lines and humiliate themselves in front of the entire audience. Athletes might be motivated to train longer hours and be more disciplined in an effort to avoid the humiliation of an inadequate performance.

Embarrassment is just as strong of a motivator as humiliation and for many of the same reasons. Embarrassment is the feeling of painful self-consciousness, being uncomfortable or shame. It might motivate us to increased performance, avoidance of behaviors that might be perceived as unacceptable, keep us out of circumstances that might put us at emotional risk, or keep us safe from scrutiny by our peers.

We have discussed physical and emotional pain as motivators; now let's take a look at how pleasure can motivate us to change.

Pleasure

- *Birth of a child*
- *Being listened to*
- *New relationships*
- *Praise & recognition*
- *Motivational speaker*
- *Cash or non-cash rewards*

Let's say you are a woman who loves a good martini after work and on the weekends with your husband. You find out you're pregnant and the doctor has suggested that you give up your cosmos and lemon drops throughout your pregnancy in order to keep your baby healthy. The joy of pregnancy and anticipation of the **birth of a child** might be the motivation you need to give up something you enjoy.

One of the top motivators for people is the simple act of **being listened to**, whether it is an employee, peer, child, significant other or friend. Simply taking the time to sit, be present, and actively listen can motivate them towards positive behaviors. As an example, if you have an employee who is under-performing, ask them what they need to be more successful or what you could do to assist them, and then listen intently to their answers. Ask a few questions but let them do most of the talking because many people just want to be heard. Maybe lean in towards them, take a few notes to show you are paying attention but stay present in the conversation. Many times the person will walk away more motivated because they will feel their opinion was valued.

New relationships can spice up our lives sometimes and give us some new motivation for change. Let's say you are single and a smoker, and you just met someone fabulous, but they mentioned that they are not only a non-smoker, but they would never date a smoker. You might decide that this relationship is so important to you that you are willing to give up your ten-year habit of smoking. It might have even been something you have tried to stop many times before and failed, but the potential for a great future with this person is a big enough motivator to help you succeed this time.

Praise and recognition is still one of the top motivators for people, especially employees and children. With that said, everyone wants praise and recognition regardless of our age, so it is powerful for most anyone. Praise breeds change, and if you praise good behavior or performance, it will motivate a person to want to do more of the same, so they can have more praise. If you ask employees what will motivate them, they will normally say "more money," but once you give it to them, what do they want the very next day? More money! What employees truly want is to be recognized and appreciated on a consistent basis with praise, and that is a much larger motivator than money for most people.

If you have ever seen a great **motivational speaker** like Zig Ziglar or Tony Robbins speak; you might have been motivated to run to the back of the room after they were done and buy hundreds of dollars of audio programs and books. Motivational speakers can motivate us to change, and if you think about what drove you to the back of the room after their speech or what behavior of theirs motivated you to action, it was more than likely their passion. Most great motivational speakers will be defined by their passion or enthusiasm for their subject matter, and that is what motivates attendees towards change.

As we discussed earlier, there is always the misperception that cash is king and that it will motivate people, which we now know is not true for most. **Non-cash awards** can be great motivators for people, and in recent years, have become more popular. As an example, you have employees who have been working long hours for months, and they are not only exhausted, but they are not keeping up very well with their personal lives either. You might create an incentive for them by setting a particular goal to meet for the month, and if they achieve that goal, you will send a house cleaner to their home to clean their house. It might cost you $120 for the service, but to the person who has no time, the perceived value is huge. Time off has also become a large motivator because most people have so little time in their lives that giving someone a half-day off or letting them come in late a couple of days can be a major motivator.

After hearing about pleasure and pain as emotional motivators, which one do you think is the bigger motivator for most people? If you guessed "Emotional pain," you would be right. Unfortunately, the perception of emotional pain can control and dominate our lives. As you will learn in this book, it does not even have to be real emotional pain; it can simply be the threat or fear of the pain that motivates us to action or in-action. Once you learn to manage your fears, having an extraordinary career and life, and achieving your greatest desires, is within your grasp.

Chapter 4

UNDERSTANDING FEAR

The definition of fear is "the anticipation of pain." It is not actually the physical or emotional pain itself that puts us into fear mode; it is simply the anticipation of the pain that drives the emotion. Fear can be difficult to diagnose in ourselves because it may mask itself as other symptoms. When we are in fear mode, we sometimes don't attach the word "fear" to it because it can come to us delivered in a different package, such as any one of the following:

- *Anger*
- *Panic*
- *Control*
- *Anxiety*
- *Jealousy*
- *Obsession*
- *Depression*
- *Pessimism*
- *Nervousness*
- *Apprehension*
- *Perfectionism*

As an example, you are outside working on the front yard, and your young children are there with you playing kickball with each other. They are having a great time kicking the ball to each other and running around the yard. You warn them to be careful and not get anywhere near the street because it is a busy road with lots of traffic. One of the children accidentally kicks the ball off the side of their foot, and the ball rolls toward the street and between two parked cars. You look up just in time to see one of them running for the ball between the two cars and heading into the street as a car is quickly approaching. Your heart races, you jump to your feet, and you yell at the child at the top of your lungs to stop. You are **angry** because the child did not heed your earlier warning. You are feeling angry because the child put you in a state where you were anticipating the pain of the injury or possible death of your loved one.

Your 1-year-old child is crawling around on the floor of the living room playing with toys that you have chosen as safe. You have proactively bought toys large enough, so they won't fit into the child's mouth and strong enough, so pieces won't break off that they might swallow. Your child sees something shiny under the sofa and goes to inspect as you are doing the dishes in the adjoining room. It is a coin that probably fell out of someone's pocket as they were seated on the sectional sofa and found its way between the cracks of the sections and to the floor below. The curious child reaches under the couch, grabs the coin and does what many young children do: they put it in their mouth. You hear a crying sound coming from the living room, see the child gasping for air, and you go into **panic** mode. You rush over to the child, pick them up and realize they have something stuck in their throat. You turn the child over, pound on their back with your open hand until the coin falls out. Your child is now safe, but the panic you felt was simply the anticipation of pain at the thought of your child suffocating.

Approximately 20 percent of the people I meet in my line of work who are in leadership roles have **control** issues of some sort. About

10 percent of those people would be what many would call "control freaks," which means they, more than likely, also have compulsive behaviors. Controllers normally want things done the way <u>they</u> want them done and when <u>they</u> want them done. As an example, you tell one of your employees that you want them to build a spreadsheet in Excel showing the comparative sales of each product for the year. You show them the way that you have always done it, with the type of bar chart you have always used before and tell them you want it by the end of the day. At noon, the employee shows up at your office and they completed the project, but they found a faster way to do it and a bar chart that shows the comparatives even better. This action makes you angry because even though it is done hours faster and with better results, they did not follow your instructions, which makes you fear you might be losing control over this employee. Their actions might also give you **anxiety** because you are now worried about what else they might change in the future. In other words, even though you have felt no pain from their actions, you are anticipating potential future pain and/or a loss of control.

I mentioned in the last paragraph that some people who are controllers may also be compulsive about their behaviors. This is probably best defined as a person with an obsessive compulsive disorder, and if you are one of them, you are probably aware of it. If not, let me give you an example: You keep a meticulous home and everything must be in its place. The driveway is swept, you could eat off the garage floor, the carpets are vacuumed perfectly, and there is no dust to be found anywhere. Everything has a place, so there is nothing on the counters or table-tops that does not belong there. You have friends over for a party, and one of them sets their glass on the coffee table without a coaster, and it gives you such angst that you rush over to put one under it. You see another guest accidentally drop a potato chip on the carpet, and your anxiety builds, so all you can focus on is that chip that needs to be picked up. If you want to know if you are one of these people, place a half empty glass on any table in the house, and leave it there for a couple of weeks to see if it drives you crazy. This **obsessive** behavior can more than likely be attributed back to the fear of losing control. The problem is normally that you lack control over yourself, so you feel inclined to control everything around you as compensation. We will talk about this in more detail later in the book.

You got married a couple of years ago, and life seemed to be grand until you found out your spouse had been cheating on you with someone at work. You divorced and moved on with your life. You are now in a new relationship and loving life for the first time in years. It is a new beginning for you with this fabulous new person who you are sure would never violate your trust like your previous spouse. You marry this person and begin enjoying a fabulous life. You stop by the office one day to visit and notice one of their co-workers, who is of the opposite sex and attractive, is laughing and joking with your significant other. Your **jealousy** boils over, and you become angry because you are revisiting the past and anticipating potential pain. You are now punishing your current spouse for the sins of your past relationship. Even though your current spouse did not commit the crime, you are sentencing them to the time because you fear it may happen again.

Depression is normally a state of unhappiness with potential symptoms of hopelessness, dejection, poor concentration, lack of energy, inability to sleep and sometimes suicidal tendencies. It can come about because of the fear of rejection, failure, embarrassment, humiliation, guilt, not being good enough, not having choices in life or being trapped and frozen in time. It can sometimes simply be the fear or anticipation of these things that can drive some people into this state. Like many of the types of fear that we have talked about so far, this one is especially debilitating because we do not see it as "fear," since we are too immersed in the symptoms. There can certainly be other medical and psychological reasons for depression, so it is a vast subject, with powerful symptoms and no easy answers for many people.

Just by the sheer dictionary definition of the word **pessimism,** you can see that fear is the perpetrator: *"Tendency to expect the worst."* Pessimists live each day by anticipating pain that does not exist or may never occur, so they live in a state of self-imposed fear. This is really sad when you consider that most of the things we worry about never come true. Imagine waking up every day believing that you won't get the promotion you applied for or that the economy will never recover or that there is no one you can trust. How hard would it be to believe that you will never find true love, never be out of poverty or never be able to lose weight? Each day you wake, your thoughts are filled with the worst case scenarios, and you live in perpetual anticipation of the pain.

The dictionary definition of **nervousness** is *"having a feeling of dread or apprehension."* In fact, the dictionary mentions *"feeling nervous about meeting his parents,"* which is another great example of anticipating pain that may never come true. Many people get nervous when taking tests; even though they studied hard and know the answers they are still uncertain of the outcome (the potential pain). Parents, who are expecting a new baby, get nervous even though all the signs show it is a healthy baby. Once again, most of these "fear masks" can be defined as symptoms and not problems. Our anxiety or nervousness is simply a warning sign that we are anticipating the possibility of forthcoming pain.

Apprehension epitomizes the anticipation of pain as well. Let's say your boss stormed into the office walked by your desk and said he wanted to see you in his office at the end of the day. First, that is a cruel thing to do to anyone because it lets your imagination run wild with what possibilities could exist for why they want to see you. Unfortunately, the human brain always wants to go to the dark side, so it creates painful stories that normally do not come true. The apprehension, or anticipation of what painful experience lies ahead, can cause incredible stress for anyone.

Even though most of us should know it, many people still have not accepted the idea that humans are incapable of perfection. If you believe that humans are capable of it and you try to hold them accountable to it, you are only setting them and yourself up for failure. With that said, I do believe that humans are capable of excellence, so that is a reasonable expectation. People who seek **perfection** also fear failure, and this can be incredibly stressful. Trying to achieve something impossible, such as perfection, always keeps you guarded and anticipating the next pain, which is the next occurrence of failure. Failure for humans is not an "if", it is a "when," so it is a lot less stressful to simply accept that failure is going to occur at some point and focus your energy on at least minimizing the effects.

What I want you to develop is an awareness that fear comes in many forms and regardless of what form it takes, it can alter your feelings, thoughts and actions. Normally, fear is about something that is not necessarily imminent, and it may be about something that never comes true, but it will still alter your response to it. As you will learn in this book, unless you develop an awareness of fear and learn to manage it, it will continue to control you and keep you from greatness.

Most humans have primal fears and these two play huge roles in our lives:

- *Not having enough*
- *Not being good enough*

"Primal" means that it is one of our most significant and primary needs as humans. We have the need to want more, and we also have the need to want to be more. If you think about the word "enough" (as in "not having enough" or "not being good enough") – what is enough? Is it something that can truly be attained or is it the carrot on the stick out in front of our nose that we chase and never catch? Will General Motors ever sell enough automobiles? Will Microsoft ever be large enough? Will Donald Trump ever be rich enough? Will winning a gold medal in the Olympics be enough to satisfy an athlete and make them feel like they are good enough? We can also relate this to our personal behaviors by asking if a person who is a pleaser will ever be able to please enough. Will a person who is a controller ever have enough control to satisfy them? Will a perfectionist ever have things perfect enough? Will a person who has an addictive personality ever have enough (of whatever they are addicted to)? The answer to all of these questions is: probably not. As humans, we are wired for inadequacy, and we will, more than likely, never feel as if we have enough.

We are great consumers because we have an insatiable appetite for more. Most people today live beyond their means. If they get a raise in pay, their spending tends to increase with it because there is more money to buy more stuff. For some people this primal fear of not having enough can be dangerous because it is not just about belongings. It can turn into the desire for more liquor, drugs, sex or gambling, which may not serve them well. The feelings of not having enough can certainly account for much of the credit card and home equity debt that consumers have created over the years, and I do not see a turn-around anytime soon. The funny part about the word "enough" is who we measure ourselves against in order to determine if we have "enough." Is it the poorest of the poor? Of course not because we have more than them! We normally measure ourselves up against people who have more than us, so we will always end up not having enough compared to who we measure ourselves against. We actually set ourselves up for failure by that simple act alone, which keeps us wanting for more and feeling inadequate.

Unfortunately, the primal fear of **not having enough** has led us to the misperception that trying to have more will make us happier, which it will not. In order to live an extraordinary life, one of the first things we must come to grips with is the concept that happiness can be bought because it cannot. If you feel depressed and decide that buying a new handbag will make you happy, it may work for a few hours or days, but you only temporarily masked the pain, and it will come back eventually. Save yourself the money by focusing your time and energy on determining why you have the symptom of depression (remember – it is a symptom and not a problem for most people).

Many people take out home equity loans on their residences to buy hot tubs, boats, new cars or other things that they thought would make them happy. Now they have the stuff, but they also have more debt and more stress wrapped around their new stuff. I will guarantee that if people were brutally honest, many would tell you that the happiness they were hoping for got replaced with stress and the fear of financial insecurity. If having more things would make people happy, then why aren't rich people walking around just giddy every day? Because it doesn't work! I know more miserable rich people than you can imagine because they have tried to find happiness through "stuff," and it is a strategy that absolutely will not work in the long run.

In this book, we will talk a lot about how you can live an extraordinary life and achieve your greatest desires, as well as your intent and why you are seeking the things you are. Happiness comes from within, and I hope this book will keep you focused on the other steps required to live an extraordinary life and not just setting your desires towards possessions. If you choose to follow all the steps of this book, you will more than likely live an extraordinary life, with the end result being happiness. Once you have found happiness from within, you will hopefully find that the things in life that you desire come easier as well.

The second primal fear is "**not being good enough,**" and it is not as easy to manage because it is relentless and exists under the radar much of the time. Because of that, it tends to go undetected, and it is very hard to manage things that you are unaware of. I truly believe that awareness can bring change; so if we are aware of our thoughts, feelings and actions, we have the opportunity to manage them. As I use the word "manage," I want it made very clear that in the business world it is not your role to manage other people (because most people don't want to be managed); I would encourage you to "lead" them instead. However, the one person I would encourage you to manage is yourself – your thoughts, feelings and actions.

The fear of not being good enough is a typical fictional story that we have fabricated in our head. These are the feelings that create low self-worth in people, but self-worth is simply a self-perception and not necessarily a reality. The problem is that once we create the perception, we develop a loyalty to it, and we replay the story over and over again in our head until we believe the story. We actually lose the ability to determine what is a story and what is reality because it becomes so real to us over time. Coming up in a few chapters, we will focus on the truth about you. We will even create a new script in your head around the truth, which will be the start to a new future for you. Since the world seems to revolve around acronyms, especially in the business world, I want to offer you one for the word F.E.A.R. However, I want you to know that I researched where this acronym originally came from, and I could not locate the source, so my apologies to the creator for not giving you credit, whoever you are:

The fear of not being good enough is atypical fictional story that we have fabricated in our head.

False

Evidence

Appears

Real

No thought lives rent free in your head, and these fears of "not having enough" or "not being good enough" are two of the biggest obstacles to you living an extraordinary life and achieving your greatest desires. Much of this book is going to focus on helping you overcome and manage these feelings because unless you learn to manage them, they will continue to manage you. How sad that something, which is normally untrue about ourselves, controls and dominates our thoughts and actions to the point that they become the glass ceiling over our head that keeps us from greatness. The great news is you can change that starting today!

So, the question is; can you eliminate fear from your life?

- *Would having control eliminate fear from your life?*
- *Would having more stuff eliminate the fear of not having enough?*
- *Would having fame eliminate the fear of not being good enough?*
- *Would having more money eliminate the fear of not having enough?*
- *Would having success eliminate the fear of not being good enough?*

I am sorry to say "No" on all counts because if you get all the money you want, then you may begin to fear losing it. If you get all the stuff you want, then you may begin to fear losing your stuff. If you achieve all the success you want, then you may begin to fear losing your success. If you achieve all the fame you want, then you may begin to fear losing your fame. If you achieve total control, then you may begin to fear losing control. You cannot eliminate fear because it is innate within us and primal in nature, so it is with us for the long haul. However, with that said, you can certainly learn to manage your fear, and I can offer you an exercise to assist with just that.

In order to demonstrate how effective this exercise is, I would like you to place yourself in a state of fear for the next ten seconds. I would like you to think about something that you fear, which will put you into an emotional state of pain. This might be the loss of a loved one, a state of humiliation or embarrassment for something that you have done, or something that makes your heart race and creates anxiety in you. Let the anxiety and fear build so you truly feel emotional about it.

Now, at the end of the ten seconds, I would like you to replace that painful thought with someone or something that you are grateful for. Think about a person or a pet in your life, a circumstance or maybe a recent event about which you truly felt grateful. It needs to be authentic gratitude where you feel the emotion behind it.

What did you notice? It should have been like a light switch where your brain and body moved from a state of fear to a state of gratitude in an instant – the fear is gone! The brain does not have the capacity to hold fear and gratitude in the same space. It is either going to be one or the other, so if you wake up in the morning with a symptom of fear such as anger, panic, anxiety, jealousy, obsession, depression, pessimism, nervousness, apprehension, or perfectionism, take a moment to take a deep breath and think about something you are grateful for, and you may find temporary relief. I used the word "temporary" because in most cases you are alleviating the symptom, but not the problem. Once you are calmed down from the exercise, it will allow you to focus on what the "problem" is, so you can address that directly. In the exercise, you may also use the emotion of "love" in place of gratitude, which will do the same thing. Now that you are aware of the outcome, I would like you to repeat the exercise and pay closer attention to the switch-like action of the brain and how fast it changes from pain to pleasure.

Fear causes trauma to your cardiovascular system that can even lead to strokes or heart attacks for some people. I have also learned through the Seattle Cancer Care Alliance that stress is one of the top triggers for cancer (smoking is right up there with it). The feelings of gratitude and love bring the cardiovascular system into a more relaxed and tranquil state, and it is that calm, which can provide many health benefits to your body. This is the same reason that prayer, meditation, yoga and positive thoughts have been proven to provide healing effects on the body and have led to many miracles where people have been completely cured of their illnesses. It is not the prayer, meditation or yoga itself that heals; it is their effect on your cardiovascular system from those actions.

Understanding how our brain works can help us manage fear, so let's talk a bit more about it before moving away from the subject of fear. If you were to go back over a couple hundred million years (give or take a year or two), you might find that some of the first creatures to roam the earth were reptiles. Their world was full of predators, so I am sure they were probably viewed as some other creature's next meal throughout much of their day. When the grass moved around them or they heard a rustling in the bushes, they would probably go into a state of heightened awareness. However, their brains were relatively limited in terms of responses because they were incapable of processing emotion or becoming analytical, so being logical was not even an option. Their brains limited them to three instinctual responses, which were:

Reptilian responses to danger (fear):

1. *Freeze*
2. *Flee*
3. *Fight*

Today, many refer to the reptile's brains as the "Reptilian Brain." Even today, reptiles are still incapable of logic or emotion and they must rely simply on instinctual primal reactions. This is why reptiles don't necessarily make great pets for people who want their adorable little creatures to meet them at the door and greet them with love and admiration. You can stand at that door as long as you want but a reptile is not going to get giddy about you or provide you with any emotional offerings because they are incapable of such things.

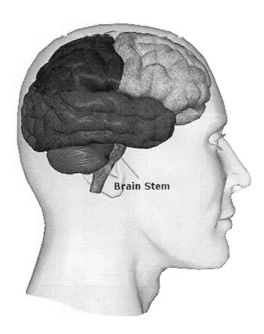

Brain Stem

The base of the Brain Stem connects to the Spinal Cord. The Brain Stem is sometimes referred to as the "Reptilian Brain."

As humans, we are very lucky because our brains have evolved over time and have given us the gifts of thought, intellect and emotion. With that said, humans actually have a part of their brain, which is referred to as the Reptilian Brain that includes the brain stem and cerebellum. It sits right on top of the spinal cord and is always on guard and scanning the environment for potential threats. This part of the brain controls normal involuntary behavior that the conscious mind does not. It monitors our survival needs and controls the body's vital functions such as:

- *Breathing*
- *Digestion*
- *Heart rate*
- *Circulation*
- *Body temperature*
- *Movement, posture and balance*

The Reptilian Brain is very good at making quick decisions based on the limited and sometimes untimely information being fed to it in dangerous or fearful situations. This part of the brain thrives in emergency situations when the thinking part of our brain does not have the time to process the threat, such as in our quick reaction to swerve in order to avoid a car accident. Our Reptilian Brain has similar responses to those of reptiles, so humans can also be prone to the three instinctual fear responses of freeze, flee and fight if put into a situation of fear. Sometimes those three options are good but sometimes they can be bad because the response may not provide the correct action based on their knee jerk reaction. The Reptilian Brain can override the more rational functions of the brain and result in unpredictable and primitive behavior, which many people may regret later. This is why it is best to think things through and give yourself time to process information before responding. The more emotionally charged you are, the more the Reptilian Brain is in charge of your thoughts and actions. Have you ever responded to an E-mail in anger and then re-read your response the next day once you were calmed down and wished you had not sent it?

As mentioned, humans have evolved beyond the Reptilian Brain, so we are fortunate to have what is called the "Mammalian Brain." The Mammalian Brain is comprised of the structures of the limbic system, which include the hippocampus, amygdale and hypothalamus. It records memories of emotional events or behaviors, good or bad, so it is responsible for many human emotions. This part of the brain is the area of value judgment that either consciously or unconsciously has a strong influence on our behaviors, and it controls functions such as:

- *Mood*
- *Motivation*

- *Hormonal secretion*
- *Emotional responses*
- *Pain & pleasure sensations*

The newest part of the human brain is called the Neocortex (neo meaning "new"), which did not develop until about 40,000 years ago (it seems like it was just yesterday). This part of the brain evaluates information from both the Reptilian and Mammalian Brains. If we end up in a state of fear and don't take reasonable time to process the flow of information, we are prone to reacting with our automated responses from the Reptilian Brain, which will try to offer us only the freeze, flee and fight options. When in a fearful situation or under stress, it is important to take a deep breath, think your response through thoroughly and maybe even sleep on it overnight if time allows. Give yourself adequate time to fully utilize your entire brain, otherwise your response may cause misguided reactions, which can waste time and drain you of energy. The Neocortex is sometimes referred to as the rational part of the brain, and it controls functions such as:

- *Reasoning*
- *Imagination*
- *Human Language*
- *Conscious thought*
- *Abstract thought (ideas)*
- *Motor commands (such as sight, sound and touch)*
- *Intellect(such as reading, writing and math calculations)*

In short, the Reptilian Brain, Mammalian Brain and Neocortex can all work together when you are put into a state of fear (when you are anticipating pain). Understanding how your brain works is important because it is entirely in control of you and the decisions you make. Taking risks or wanting to change is going to put you into a state of anticipated pain, so your brain will try to keep you from these things. If you plan on living an extraordinary life and achieving your greatest desires, you are going to have to learn to manage what goes on in your brain. You have heard me say it many times before: if you do not learn how to manage it, it will continue to manage you, and you will be hard pressed to fulfill your dreams and desires.

Here is a good question for you: Is there any possibility that your lack of desire is directly related to the fear of emotional pain? In other words, are you sabotaging yourself and your desires because of your fear of failure, rejection, embarrassment or humiliation if you attempt and do not succeed in achieving your desires? Is it possible that you will never allow your desires to become the "Most important" to you because the word "Most" makes you accountable and commits you to action? I truly believe that this is one of the biggest reasons why many people never achieve their desires. Fear can create inaction in many people because they try to protect themselves from emotional pain, which means they will never fully commit to their desires.

It is interesting that we are taught in school that failure is a horrible thing that is measured daily in our grades (you got a failing grade or you failed the test), in sports (you failed to make the shot, failed to make the team or failed to win) and in life (you failed your driving test or failed to live up to our expectations). I wish we could learn to either remove the word from our vocabulary or at least re-frame it, so it does not become such an emotional wound for people.

If you look back through time, you can find examples such as Thomas Edison who tried 1,400 experiments before he was able to make the light bulb work properly. Did he fail 1,400 times or did he learn 1,400 lessons? If he had viewed those as 1,400 failures, my guess is that you would be reading this book in the dark because he would have struggled pretty hard getting up every day to work on a project on which he failed that many times. My guess is that he viewed them as 1,400 lessons, which got him closer to his goal each day. I am also going to guess that each successful experiment helped build his confidence and motivated him to continue his journey. If we could all re-frame our lives in that manner, then maybe the "fear" of failure would not be so disabling that it keeps us from greatness.

Have you ever watched a 1-year-old toddler trying to walk for the first time? They wobble across the floor weaving from side to side until they fall face first into the carpet. What do they do next? They get back up, re-adjust and try it again. They don't feel like they failed, and they don't beat themselves up over it; they learn from their experiences and get back at it. Each time they repeat the process and get closer to success, it builds their confidence and motivates them to keep trying. As we get older, that innocence escapes us for some reason, and we turn events like that into emotional pain and feelings of failure. This drives our self-worth into the ground and makes us want to quit trying in order to protect ourselves emotionally. We should never lose that child-like ability to attempt new things, and if we are not successful, we need to get back up and do it again without beating ourselves up. We need to find ways to build our confidence and stop inhibiting ourselves through self-doubt.

You have probably heard of the old saying "*The rich get richer, and the poor get poorer.*" Do you believe that? Parts of it are true because some people in this world have a greater tolerance for taking risks (based on their level of confidence), and they are rewarded for their efforts. Those who are not willing to take risks will not advance in life as quickly. Do you know how many millions of people have great ideas but never execute them because they have a fear of the unknown or they fear failure, rejection, humiliation or embarrassment? There are certainly far more people like that than the ones who are willing to throw caution to the wind and push forward with innovative ideas even in the face of danger.

Imagine a person, whom we shall call Bob, who has very little money, but a great new idea for a product that will save people hours of time each day. Bob tells his friends and family about the idea, but his ingenuity is dismissed as a far-fetched dream. He works hard to earn enough money to build a couple dozen of his product and he takes an emotional risk by approaching a local store owner to buy his product. It is such a hit with the customers that the store owner orders more. Bob is beaming with confidence, so he takes another risk and finds a company to manufacture his product for him. It is a risk because he has to order 1,000 at a time in order for this company to make the product for him. He accepts the risk and decides he better get out and sell to other stores, since he has 1,000 of them on order that will be delivered soon.

The 1,000 units sell, and his confidence is even stronger, so he takes another risk by creating another product that complements the one he already has. It too becomes a success and in turn it motivates him to expand his options and take even more risks. So, is it possible that the rich get richer simply because they were willing to take risks initially, and with each success, their confidence grew and motivated them to take more risks? Each success created more wealth, but it was not the money that built Bob's confidence, it was both his ability to manage fear and the rewards in accepting risk.

Is it possible that the poor get poorer because they lack confidence and therefore have a lower tolerance for accepting risk? If you have very little money, just like Bob, but have no confidence and are not willing to take some risk, especially emotional risk, how will you move from where you are today? I think the problem gets worse and perpetuates itself over time. For example, if you already have low self-confidence, and you lose your job, it might drive your self-confidence even further down. Each month you are out of work, you begin to further question your self-worth, which can make you feel even more undervalued in the world and drive you deeper into despair. Unlike the case of Bob (who took risk, built his confidence over time and created wealth), we can also freeze ourselves in a place and time by our deteriorating confidence and drive ourselves into a state of poverty, helplessness and depression.

I said a few paragraphs ago that parts of the statement, "*The rich get richer and the poor get poorer*" are true. I believe half of the statement, but not all of it and here is the reason why. I believe that the rich, based on their growing confidence, do get richer. However, I do not believe the poor get poorer; the gap between the rich and poor just grows with time. If the rich are getting richer and the poor continue on their path, then their income levels will grow apart as shown below.

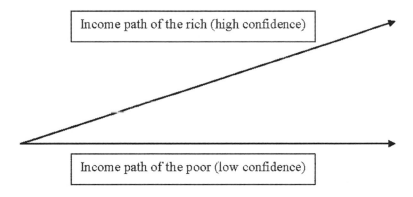

Income path of the rich (high confidence)

Income path of the poor (low confidence)

People willing to take risks are more likely to get rewarded with increased wealth (and confidence).

For years, there have been many well intended politicians who have attempted to re-distribute wealth through legislation. They believe that the world's problems would be solved if we could take money from the rich and give it to the poor. Wealth re-distribution can come in many forms, but the most popular is to tax the rich and give tax or financial benefits to the poor. It is really easy to do because 95 percent of the population isn't considered rich, and it does not negatively impact them, so of course taxing the rich sounds good to many people. However, if you take money from the rich and gave it to the poor, does that truly solve our problems and help those in need?

Before I go any further, I would like you to know that I am taking a broad brush stroke to the words "rich" and "poor" because they are almost impossible to define. There is no standardized definition for those two words because they are simply a perception based on your own circumstance. Also, they do not have to be attached to money because I consider myself incredibly rich, but it is more about love and gratitude.

If we were to talk strictly about money, a Gallup poll in 2003 found that the public's median definition of rich was an income of $120,000 or assets of $1 million. When MSN Money readers were asked the same question, they felt that it would take $5 million to be considered rich. I have heard many people say that anyone making twice as much as they are is rich. So, if you make $30,000 a year, you might consider anyone making over $60,000 as rich. If you make $60,000 a year, you might consider anyone making over $120,000 a year as rich.

The Federal Government, as of the writing of this book, is talking about increasing taxes on any family making over $250,000 a year in order to help pay down our national debt because they believe that is the measure of "rich." As of the writing of this book, Washington State is considering a "rich tax" on any single person making over $200,000 per year, or $400,000 for a family in order to help solve the state's budget dilemma. However, if you ask Bill Gates, Paul Allen, Warren Buffett or Donald Trump what rich is, you will be talking billions. So, "rich" and "poor" are simply a moving target based on who you talk to, and as I use those words, please know that they are simple terms for a complex conversation.

Let's just say that you take enough money from the rich, so each poor person gets a one-time check for $100,000 to help kick start them toward financial freedom. What do you think would happen to that money in most cases? Based on one of our primal fears as humans (not having enough), I am going to anticipate that there would be some pent up purchasing in an attempt to make the recipients happy. People who are unhappy will buy something they believe will make them happy, and that will suffice for a few days until that happiness wears off. Then they will buy something else to help make them happy, and the trend will continue until the money is gone. It is the same addiction as alcohol and drugs for some people because they think those things will make them happy. It makes them happy for a short time, but as soon as the buzz wears off, you need more to make you happy. The good news is that the $100,000 per person program would ccrtainly put a lot of money back into the economy quickly since they will spend most of it in short order.

I would argue that these people don't need money; they need confidence, and giving people something for nothing will not achieve that. People who get saved do not become happier and they do not become more confident. Quite the opposite, they continue to question their self-worth, fill themselves with more self-doubt and destroy any remaining confidence they might have had. Giving people something for nothing might make us all feel good in that we at least made an attempt to help the poor, but the end result would be horrible.

Now, let's look at what that $100,000 would do if it stayed in the hands of a rich person. More than likely, that money would be re-invested back into their business to help it grow, so they could buy more equipment and tools, which would help keep money in the economy and stimulate more jobs. As their business grows, it would require them to hire more employees and put more people back to work. It would also help pay for employee benefits such as medical, dental, life insurance, 401K, profit sharing, paid vacations and other employee values.

Most of the "rich" people today are self-employed small to medium-sized business owners and they are not hoarding wealth; they are building wealth through their businesses. $100,000 in these hands translates into the long term annuity of jobs, benefits and cash into the economy. This does not mean that we should stop trying to find ways to help people who are less fortunate build better lives, but it needs to happen by building their confidence. We need to keep people working and gaining confidence, so they can learn to manage fear and find their own way to building wealth. It is truly sad that the biggest thing standing between the rich and the poor is simply their level of confidence and self-worth.

My point is that we need to stop beating ourselves up emotionally and stop letting fear dominate and control our lives. Success is not about being smarter or having more money, it is about believing in yourself and giving up self-doubt. Self-worth and confidence are simply perceptions we have about ourselves, but they often become a reality that we develop loyalty to. Regaining your self-worth and confidence is about taking emotional risks and doing things that others are not willing to do in order to have the things that others do not have. It is about building confidence by taking some risk and showing success. I have always lived by the theory that the biggest risks can bring the biggest rewards. I have left nothing on the table in this world and will go to my grave never regretting or wishing that I would have tried something or done something that I did not do. I will tell you that I have taken many risks over my life (financial, physical and emotional); some have paid off and others not. However, if looking at the big picture, the risks have paid huge dividends in helping me have an extraordinary career and life, and achieve my greatest desires.

Chapter 5

THE PARALYSIS OF VICTIMIZATION

Being a victim starts when you let primal fear take over and freeze you in a specific place and time. You replay "your story" in your head and fall prey to wanting someone else to fix your problem, which sabotages your personal power. You are frozen in time; crying out for help; waiting to be rescued, and it requires no action on your part. The bottom line: feeling like a victim is a choice and an extremely poor one at that.

Some people choose to spend their days coming up with excuses as to why they cannot make more money, get the promotion they have always wanted, own a home, start a new business or have a great relationship. The dialogue in their head is a list of all the reasons (which are actually excuses that they mask as reasons) why things cannot be done and how they have no control over many of those things. There is certainly some reality to the fact that there are some things we have no control over individually, like the weather, tides, economy, other people's behaviors, et cetera. But instead of freezing yourself in time with what you can't do (which is what victims tend to do), spend time thinking about what you can do. The shift in energy from "*I can't*" to "*I can*" is huge, and it can move people forward to living extraordinary lives and achieving their greatest desires. Choose to take responsibility for the things you can control and empower yourself toward action!

There is a cute story I heard a long time ago about four little frogs that are walking down a muddy road as they head to the park to play. They are talking and laughing and not paying much attention to where they are going when one of the frogs falls into a deep tire rut in the muddy road. He tries to get out on his own as his friends look on. He asks them for help and even though the other three frogs try to help him, he keeps falling back into the muddy rut. It seems that the more they try to help, the harder it gets for the little frog to get out. His three friends tell the little frog that they're going to the park, to play for a while, and on their way back, they would gather some sticks that might help him get out. The three little frogs are at the park playing for about 10 minutes when all of a sudden the little frog that was stuck shows up. They ask him how he got out and he says, "*I had to, there was a truck coming.*"

I think all of us know someone who we feel sorry for and that we have tried to help out. But no matter what we do, they seem to fall deeper into their rut and continue to ask others to save them. If you are a person who always needs to be saved, how do you feel about yourself? What happens to your self-worth when you believe that you have become incapable of surviving on your own? It obviously drives your self-worth even lower and perpetuates your own negative self-perception. Your personal power is gone; you feel trapped, and you are ripe for a deep form of depression.

Here are three things to remember in life and business:

- *Never act like a victim*

- *Never wait to be rescued*

- *Never look for someone to blame*

I would like victims to give up their way of thinking for a number of reasons, but mostly because they are truly capable of so much more. It is easy to blame someone else for your failures or the situation you are in. If we can make someone else wrong, it makes us feel right, which feels pretty good if you are feeling down about yourself. Being a victim is a very lazy choice because it requires no action on your part. If you feel there is nothing you can do, then you don't have to do a thing! If you feel that where you are in your life is the result of someone else's action, then you might choose to dismiss any personal responsibility. If you are waiting to be rescued from your circumstances, then you can just sit back and wait to be saved. If you don't get saved, then that is certainly someone's fault for not helping you, and you can jump back in to the cycle of blaming your family, friends, coworkers or supervisor for their inaction.

> *Being a victim is a very lazy choice because it requires no action on your part.*

Pay attention to your thoughts, behaviors and beliefs. If any of the above victimization thoughts cross your mind, be aware of them and re-frame them to accept personal responsibility. Uncertainty kills dreams and destroys confidence, especially uncertainty about yourself. It is your life, and you are in charge of it. Are you waiting for someone to write the script of your life or are you going to do it yourself? Never give anyone that much power over your life – you are the only one that should be writing that script, so start today with a clean sheet of paper and make it an Academy Award winner. Personal power is the only path to having an extraordinary career and life and achieving your greatest desires.

Chapter 6

YOUR INNER SABOTEUR

I have always loved the quote, "No thought lives rent-free in your head" because we all have thoughts rolling around in our heads, but for some of us they are empowering, and for others, they are disempowering. Everyone has an inner saboteur or voice in their head that attempts to thwart their best efforts to live an extraordinary life and achieve their greatest desires. I refer to this inner voice as the Gremlin.

The term "Gremlin" is said to have originated in the Royal Air Force back in the first half of the 1900s. It was known as a mischievous trickster that got blamed for unexplained mechanical difficulties with their airplanes during the war. The Gremlin became a popular explanation for something unknown that was sabotaging their flying missions by fouling the mechanics of their planes. It is also theorized by some that the term "Gremlin" came from the old English word "Gremian" which meant "to vex." Gremlins were portrayed as equal opportunity saboteurs, taking no sides in conflict and simply acting out and causing grief for their own self-interests, which is what they still do to each and every one of us. The Gremlin went on to be portrayed in movies and books as a cute but mischievous little creature that loved to create chaos. Regardless of how you want to portray or visualize this inner saboteur, you have one.

I will use the word "Gremlin" metaphorically to encompass the internal perceptions, thoughts and feelings about ourselves that can disempower us. Perceptions, however, are just beliefs about ourselves that we develop loyalty to. The Gremlin is always there to point out your beliefs about your weaknesses, your fears and your failures, and it will be with you the rest of your life, 24 hours-a-day and 7 days-a-week. It loves to remind you about any emotional wounds from the past. The Gremlin will attempt to sabotage you by whispering self-limiting thoughts into your ear.

It is unfortunate that our brain processes a tremendous amount of information per second (billions of bits), but so much of it is negative. As an example, if your child is always home from school at 3 p.m. and you notice it is now 3:15, what does your brain do? It goes into panic mode and creates a story that is normally not true. As another example, your husband calls you at 5 p.m. and tells you that he has to work late tonight with his secretary, so what does your brain do? It goes right to the dark side. Even though you may trust him, your brain loves to tell dark stories to instill fear into you. It is interesting that our Gremlin works so hard at creating fictitious stories, and we tend to believe them, when truly most of the things we worry about never come true. My encouragement to you is to remember this when thrust into a state of fear, revert back to this moment, back yourself off the emotional cliff and process the information you have available to you. Ask yourself if the story in your head is the Gremlin's perverted storyline or are you dealing with quantifiable facts?

Before we go any further, I am going to try to give the Gremlin some credit for having our best interests in mind at times in our lives. The Gremlin has a goal of trying to keep us physically and emotionally safe. It may have saved our lives many times with its inner voice that tries to warn us of impending danger. As an example, if you were snowboarding down the mountain on a beautiful sunny day, you might have noticed a huge jump approaching. Your initial reaction is *"Cool! I will pick up more speed and hit that jump as fast as I can and get big air."* This is the point where your Gremlin chimes in and you hear the inner voice that says *"Whoa tiger! Slow it down a bit. Don't you think it would be a good idea to check out the landing first to make sure there are no tree stumps or people in the way?"* What a nice Gremlin! It is trying to serve you here by keeping you safe from physical pain.

As another example, you are riding around in your new car late one evening with friends showing off this 400 horsepower beast that can leave a strip of rubber a block long. You get to a straight stretch of road, and your friends challenge you to see if you can get the car up over 100 miles per hour. Just before you mash the gas pedal into the floor mat and go for the gusto, your Gremlin speaks up and says, *"Did you know that if a tire blows out at 100 miles per hour, your car will more than likely roll out of control, and there is a huge likelihood that you will all die?"* See, once again, what a nice Gremlin to throw a little warning flag up and try to keep you safe from physical harm.

The Gremlin also tries diligently to protect us from impending emotional pain, but here is where its exuberance begins to thwart our growth and desires to live an extraordinary life. It will try to throw caution at you by challenging your desired actions and offering you words of self-doubt such as:

- *"But, what if....?"*
- *"This is too risky"*
- *"You're not ready"*
- *"You're not worthy"*
- *"You're not pretty enough"*
- *"You're not smart enough"*
- *"What if this doesn't work?"*
- *"We have never done this before"*

One of the Gremlin's favorite phrases is, *"But, what if"* because it can be used in so many different circumstances. Let's just say you want to ask your boss for a promotion, which you truly deserve, and you can even quantify it. You have worked 20 hours of overtime each week in order to help others on your team. You are personally responsible for a 10 percent increase in revenue for your department, and you are on target for a record year. Your co-workers like you, your supervisor likes you, and there should be no reason why you would not get the promotion if you asked for it. You arrive at work with complete confidence, and this is the day that you are going in your supervisor's office to make your request. Then, a little voice in your head says, *"But what if they say no? Maybe they won't think I am ready for the responsibility yet or maybe Bob in accounting will get it because he is smarter than me. What if everyone finds out I asked for the promotion and I do not get it? That would be embarrassing."* Your enthusiasm is now crushed. Your confidence is waning and you decide you had better sleep on it because you don't want to put yourself into a situation that might be embarrassing or make you feel humiliated. You retreat back to emotional safety and why? Because a little voice in your head filled you with self-doubt when there was no need for it.

Let's say you have been working for the same printing company for 20 years, and the owner decides he wants to sell his business and retire. You know the business inside and out, and there is no part of the industry that you cannot handle. The owner approaches you and asks if you would like to purchase the company from him, and he will make it affordable by letting you pay him over a five-year period. You look at it on paper and based on current sales and profits, you can easily make the payments to the owner, put more money in your own pocket and end up owning the business outright in five years. You excitedly go home to your family to tell them of the great opportunity that awaits you. They begin asking questions that you had not yet considered such as the risks involved and the downsides to being the owner. You go to bed that night, and your brain is about ready to explode because there are so many unanswered questions. You want the best for yourself and your family, but at what risk are you willing to take on this huge obligation? Your brain now goes to the dark side and starts inundating you with phrases such as *"This is too risky," "You're not ready," "You're not worthy," "You're not smart enough," "What if this doesn't work?"* or *"We have never done this before."* The next day the owner asks if you had a chance to sleep on it, and you turn down the opportunity of a lifetime because of an inner voice that wants to keep you unchanged because

The Gremlin has no morals, so it has no problem telling lies about you

it is emotionally safer. The Gremlin, in its selfishness, does not like change, so it is going to impose its insecurities on you and rob you of a fabulous opportunity and the potential for an extraordinary life. I will tell you that this inner voice is speaking to you and controlling you every day of your life.

Your inner voice is very powerful because it can be unforgiving, doubt producing and energy draining. It will continue to remind you of your imperfections and weaknesses, even though they may truly not be of consideration. The Gremlin has no morals, so it has no problem telling lies about you, and the worst thing is that it can be VERY convincing. It has a great story to tell, and you seem to be a great audience, so it will go deep to fabricate any story it can in order to keep you from making changes or taking action. Its goal is to keep you from changing anything because it does not like change. Uncertainty is its enemy, and if it can keep you the way you are, then it has won (unfortunately, you lose).

The Gremlin's primary methodology is to instill fear into you, to scare you into conformity and to convince you to back down from trying new things. One of the challenges is that the Gremlin will try to mask its self-talk by trying to convince you that it has your best interests at heart. It will say it's trying to protect you from physical, or more often, emotional pain (as if it is helping you), but it is actually trying to frighten and threaten you with possible risk such as:

- *What if you fail?*
- *What if you are wrong?*
- *What if you get rejected?*
- *What if you get humiliated?*
- *What if you get embarrassed?*

You only have one Gremlin, but it has many voices and will try to reinforce many of your emotional wounds from the past when presented with an opportunity. As an example, a 13-year-old boy named Jim goes to his first junior high dance, and he is so excited he can hardly stand it. This is a chance to show everyone that he has smooth moves and is a dancing machine. The music has been playing for about 30 minutes, but everyone is afraid to be the first one on the dance floor, so it remains empty. Jim decides to take an emotional risk, so he tells his entourage of friends that he is going to get this dance ramped up by walking across the dance floor to ask the most beautiful girl in school to dance. His friends show their support and encourage him to make his move. Jim takes off and walks all the way across the huge empty dance floor and approaches the girl of his dreams. He politely asks her to dance in front of all her friends, and she turns to him and says, "*I don't think so!*" and then turns away from him. Now, Jim has to walk back across that huge dance floor alone, back to all his friends who are watching this train wreck unfold and try to explain why he just got rejected. Think of the humiliation, embarrassment and feelings of rejection he must be feeling.

You have to know that Jim isn't even going to a dance for the next five or ten years, let alone ask a girl to dance. Matter of fact, fast-forward 30 years to when Jim is 43 years old, divorced and thrust back into the single world. He is out at a bar with friends, the band is playing great music, and he sees a gorgeous woman that he would love to dance with. Just about the time he gets the nerve to walk over to her, his Gremlin pops up and says to him, *"Whoa big Jim, do you remember the last time you asked a girl to dance? Do you remember that junior high dance and how embarrassing and humiliating that was? Why would you put yourself through that again?"* Jim retreats back to the safety of his bar stool in order to protect himself from the emotional pain of embarrassment, humiliation or rejection. The Gremlin is relentless and will continue to haunt Jim and try to protect him from that specific emotional pain for the rest of his life. You can see how the Gremlin, in its exuberance, will become a detriment to Jim because it will never allow Jim to heal that wound. It will possibly impede on his finding a great relationship because he will be unwilling to take any emotional risk. The Gremlin will remind him of it for the rest of his life, which will limit him and keep him from living an extraordinary life.

Melanie was not much of an athlete in school. Actually, she will tell you that not only was she not an athlete, she had no physical skills to be found at all. She was the nicest person in the school yard, with a heart of gold, but an Olympic Medal was not in her future. So to say that she disliked P.E. (physical education) class would be an understatement. She told me they used to break the class up into teams to play some of the sports, whether it was baseball, basketball, dodge ball or any other team sport. The coach would designate two students as team captains, and they would take turns picking other classmates for their team. She remembers vividly being the last person picked each time. One time when Melanie was the last one standing waiting to be picked, one of the team captains got a disgusted look on their face and said in front of everyone, *"Do we have to have her again? We had her last time!"* That is a great example of an emotional wound that will stick with her for the rest of her life. Even today as an adult, when anyone talks about choosing teams, it sends shivers down her spine because the inner voice starts reminding her of the embarrassment, humiliation or rejection that she endured in school.

Most people pick up their Gremlin in their school years, probably between the ages of 7 to 15. I think it happens because kids at that age are pretty insecure about themselves as they try to discover who they are. You combine insecurity with how cruel kids can be to each other, and it is a perfect recipe for the birth of a Gremlin.

Even though I did not discover my Gremlin until I was about 46 years old, it was created when I was about 15 years old. As I mentioned in my introduction of the book, I had a lot of friends growing up, so I enjoyed school from the social standpoint. I went to all the sporting events, and if there was a party within 20 miles, I was there. Scholastically, I struggled with my grades, so I was about a "C" student. Out of embarrassment, I masked my inadequacy from my friends, so you would be hard-pressed to find anyone in school that did not believe I was an "A" or "B" student.

As I sat in classrooms, I would try very hard to pay attention to what the teacher was saying because I knew we would be tested on it, but I struggled with retaining the information. I had the same challenges with reading text books in class or at home because as I was reading, my brain kept drifting away, and I would have to re-read the same page two or three times in order to understand it. When it came time to take a test on the information that the teacher was talking about or a book that we were supposed to have read, I could not recall the answers easily. Retaining and regurgitating knowledge was not my strong suit, and I could not figure out why most other people seemed to do it with ease when I could not.

Looking back at it, I was very frustrated with myself because I was not lazy in school; I actually did try. If I would have been able to declare myself as lazy, non-caring, apathetic or disinterested, it would have been easier to understand, but when you are trying as hard as you can and failing, it can be frustrating. In my senior year, I flunked my World Problems class, which panicked me because it meant that I would not be able to graduate. I went to Grays Harbor Community College and took a night class in order to make up my credits, so I could graduate with my class. I was embarrassed that I might not graduate and about the night class, so I didn't share it with anyone. My cumulative grade point upon graduation was 2.47 (out of a possible 4.0), which is certainly not a stellar grade point average.

The answers as to why I struggled in school came later in life when my son, Tate, was diagnosed with Attention Deficit Disorder (ADD) – twice, once in grade school and a second time in junior high. I watched him suffer in school like I had. I could see his self-worth waning even though I knew he was a brilliant kid. We sought help through the school system to no avail. They claimed they had no programs to help him. Then we looked at the medical world, but that too ended in frustration because after almost a year of trying different drugs, we could not find a medication that would work for him. It was very hard for me to see him suffer. I knew his pain and completely understood how he felt. His poor grades began to shape who he thought he was (his self-image), which was far from the truth. The story in his head was that he was not smart enough, but the truth is he is very creative and extremely bright. His perceptions about himself were formed by his grades and not by his real life, just like what happened to me.

In the journey to find solutions for my son, I learned that ADD is usually hereditary. I realized that I had been the carrier of this disorder, which explained my struggle in school as well (and the same struggles my father seemed to have had before me). Without writing an entire book on this subject (which I could), the bottom line is that ADD and ADHD (Attention Deficit Hyperactivity Disorder) are not the kiss of death for anyone who has them. Those of us affected by either of them are misunderstood because the school system measures "smart" by a grade point, but thank goodness, the world outside of school measures us by our performance.

The school system frustrates the heck out of me because a child's ability seems to be measured by how well they can retain and recall information. Even to this day, I do not think they have figured out how to evaluate a student's potential or deal with students who have ADD, ADHD or many of the other learning challenges that exist. Instead of finding solutions for why so many people drop out or don't get good grades, the system in many cases redirects the blame to the students by labeling them as unmotivated, underperforming, un-teachable and lazy, or by telling them, *"You don't apply yourself."* In many cases, it's not true. Often times, the school system is ineffective, and no one seems to have the courage or ability to fix it! I know that many well intentioned people in the system have tried to improve student learning over the years, but they are putting "Band-Aids" on a severed limb – it needs a complete and comprehensive overhaul from the top down. One hundred years from now, people will look back with shame at how students were taught, evaluated and unfairly misclassified under our current grade-point system. I don't blame the teachers or administrators because they are victims of the system as well and inadequately compensated. I truly believe they do the best with what they are given; the problem is deeply systemic, and it needs to be taken apart and overhauled before we cause any more emotional damage to children.

I mentioned earlier that I graduated with a 2.47 grade point average, and my Gremlin has been working to try to convince me that I am not good enough since I was a teenager. So what is the definition of "not good enough"? According to many school systems as of the writing of this book, a 2.47 GPA (grade point average) is a grade of "C," which could be labeled "average". However, if you are a student with less than a 2.5 GPA, my guess is that you don't consider yourself anywhere close to average. More than likely, you consider yourself inadequate or not good enough, like I did.

Why? When I was in school, you had to have a 3.00 GPA in order to make the honor roll, and if you had anything less, your grades were "not good enough." Apply for a scholastic scholarship to continue your education, and you will more than likely get a letter back that says your GPA is "not good enough." Try to get into a good four year college with less than a 2.50 GPA, and you will more than likely be told that is "not good enough." Try to apply for a good paying job in the business world, and when they ask you what your GPA was in school, and you tell them a 2.47, you will find out that it is "not good enough" to get the job.

To prepare for this book, I did some research in order to find out how many people might be feeling the same way I did, which is "not good enough" due to their GPA. I was able to attain some statistics from the State of Washington for the school year 2008-2009 for grades 10, 11 and 12. Even though this is only the State of Washington, I will assume there are states that are better and worse, but I think this would be a fair representation of students throughout the United States. Below are the grade point averages and how many students in grades 10, 11 and 12 had those grades, plus how many students with those grade points dropped out and did not complete the school year:

3.50 to 4.00 GPA =	20% (.5% drop out rate)
3.00 to 3.49 GPA =	19% (1.0% drop out rate)
2.50 to 2.99 GPA =	18% (1.8% drop out rate)
2.00 to 2.49 GPA =	15% (4.0% drop out rate)
Less than 2.00 GPA =	21% (13.8% drop out rate)
Unreported GPA =	7% (18.0% drop out rate)

Not including the "Unreported" category, about 36 percent of all the students in the State of Washington in grades 10, 11 and 12 for the school year 2008 - 2009 had less than a 2.50 grade point average. That means that more than one of every three students in those three grades probably does not feel good enough. I also evaluated some specific school districts in the state, and there are some that have almost 50 percent of the students with GPAs with less than 2.50. As you can also see above, as the GPA goes down, the percentage of students who drop out goes up dramatically. Are they dropping out because they are truly not smart enough to make it through school or is it possible that they are dropping out because they do not feel good enough, based on how we teach and test children, and they have simply given up hope? Are they quitting because they are trying to protect themselves from the emotional pain of continued failure? The question from my perspective is; are the students not good enough? Or is the system not good enough? The fact that 1 in 3 kids (1 in 2 kids in some districts) are ending up with less than a 2.50 grade point average tells me that something is broken, and the students are paying the long-term price.

Why am I making an issue of the school system and grades? Because it has been the measure of success for hundreds of years, and in my opinion, it is inaccurate. If you tried hard, like I did, and did not do well in school, it is not the kiss of death for your career or life. Your grades are not a measure of your self-worth, they are a measure of your heredity and your physical ability to retain and spit out information upon command in most cases. No one should leave our school system wounded from the experience and convinced by their low grades that they are not worthy of a great future. I want you to know that regardless of your grades, you can live an extraordinary life and achieve your greatest desires, so do not let anything stand in your way!

In my leadership seminars, I teach that people do not fail as much as systems do, so I would apply the same thought here as well. If more than one of every three students leaves our school system not feeling good enough, what is this doing to their confidence? As I pointed out in an earlier chapter, confidence is one of the keys to success, so how confident can you feel with a GPA under 2.50? I just think it is sad that we are sending more than one-third of our children into the world with a Gremlin on their shoulder reminding them every single day about how they are not good enough, when it is not necessarily true. I truly believe the GPA is a poor indicator of a person's abilities or talents, and until we come up with a better system, we will continue to send emotionally damaged children into this world with a life sentence of "you're not good enough" (who simply become emotionally wounded adults).

Part of the problem with your ability to learn and retain information is physical and hereditary. It is because of a switch in your brain called the Reticular Activating System, and most people are unaware it even exists. If you ask 100 teachers or administrators if they know what the Reticular Activating System is, you might get lucky and find that one of them has even heard of it. I speak all over the world and have been asking my audiences for 20 years if they know what the Reticular Activating System is and 99 percent of the attendees have no idea that it exists. The Reticular Activating System does not just impact only a few students; it controls and dominates every one of them but certainly in different ways and on different levels.

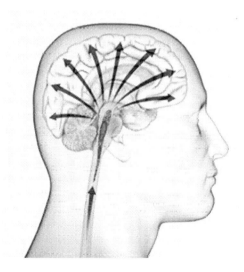

Inbound information flows through the Reticular Activating System (located inside the brain stem and mid-brain) and into other areas of the brain.

The Reticular Activating System plays a significant role in determining whether a person can learn and remember well or not and also whether they are highly motivated or bored easily. It is a loose network of neurons and neural fiber that is connected at its base to the spinal cord and runs up through the brain stem to the mid-brain. It is the center of control for other parts of the brain involved in learning, self-control or inhibitions and motivation. In short, it is the attention center of the brain, and it is the switch that turns your brain on and off. When functioning properly, it provides the connections that are needed for the processing and learning of information, plus the ability to stay focused on the correct task.

If the Reticular Activating System doesn't stimulate the neurons of the brain as much as it should, that is when people have difficulty learning, poor memory, lack of attention or self-control. If the Reticular Activating System over stimulates the brain, then that is when people become hyperactive, talk too much and become too restless. The Reticular Activating System must be activated to normal levels for the rest of the brain to function as it should. That is why many people are prescribed Ritalin and other such stimulant medications because it helps control the amount of stimulation to the brain.

The Reticular Activating System is best known as a filter because it sorts out what is important information that needs to be paid attention to and what is unimportant and can be ignored. Without this filter, we would all be over stimulated and distracted by noises from our environment around us. As an example, let's just say you were a mother who has a baby sleeping in the next room, and you live right next to a busy airport with lots of loud noise from jets taking off and landing. Despite the constant roar of the jets and other noise, you will hear your baby if it makes even the smallest noise in the next room. The Reticular Activating System filters out the airport noise, which is unimportant to you and keeps you focused on your baby, which is the "Most important" thing to you. The Reticular Activating System is like a filter between your conscious mind and your subconscious mind. It takes instructions from your conscious mind (like "*I need to hear my baby*") and passes it on to your subconscious mind, which becomes diligent and alert to your request.

In the world of learning, the Reticular Activating System is like a switch in your head that turns on and off based on how much telling tension or self-talk you have going on inside your head. If the switch is open, you can retain information easily, and if the switch is closed, you cannot. If you are sitting in a seminar bored because the person speaking is not engaging enough (your brain is not stimulated enough), your Reticular Activating System will turn off and treat the person as irritating background noise, just like the noisy airport in the previous example. We will still see the person speaking and hear their voice, but we will not retain the information.

Going back to my earlier point about the educations system: how on earth can the education system help students learn and retain information when even they don't fully understand how the brain works? I truly believe that if tested, we would find that many of the people with a GPA under 2.50 have some level of ADD or ADHD that is impeding their ability to do well in school, and both are tied to the Reticular Activating System. In other words, I think they are smart enough, but they probably don't test well because they cannot retain information and recall it upon command during tests (due to their Reticular Activating System).

The ability to retain information has nothing to do with how smart you are; it simply means you were a member of the lucky sperm club. If you look at people who did real well in school and had great grades, you can be almost certain that at least one of their parents did as well, if not both. I know people who never studied, yet they got straight "As" and in most cases, it was true of their parents as well. Those people have the gift of genealogy passed down through the family chain and their gift is a great Reticular Activating System that allows the free flow and retention of information. You cannot change your gene pool at this point because you have what you have, but you can choose how you handle what you have by knowing more about the brain and how it works.

I will give you a couple of examples of how the Reticular Activating System may have impacted you. Remember sitting in a classroom for an hour? You are almost certain the teacher was there because you could see them walking around and you could hear their voice, even though you are not certain about the message. You thought you were listening because you could see them and hear their voice. However, at the end of the class you got up, walked out the door and you have very little, if any, memory about what you learned. That is because if the teacher was not engaging enough to you, you disengaged and you began to daydream. You went to a happy place and thought about your upcoming date this weekend, your new car, or about an idea you had for a company you would like to start some day. Daydreaming is "self-talk," which shuts the Reticular Activating System off and makes it difficult for you to retain what the teacher is saying.

I will give you another example. Have you ever driven down a freeway on a sunny afternoon, daydreaming until you awaken

People with ADD and ADHD are not dumb

suddenly after five minutes realizing that you missed your exit? You don't remember cars passing you or if you passed other cars, and you don't remember what was on the radio. It should terrify you that you are a 3,000-pound missile flying down the freeway at 60 miles an hour, and you have no memory of the last five minutes of your drive. How can that possibly be? It's because day dreaming is "self-talk," which shuts down the Reticular Activating System and keeps you from remembering.

People with ADD and ADHD are not dumb, even though their grades might make them feel that way sometimes. Most are very creative, and their mind is filled with thoughts that at times shut down the Reticular Activating System and make it hard for them to retain information. However, put people with ADD or ADHD in the workplace and in most cases they function extremely well. As a matter of fact, people with ADHD can make great entrepreneurs because they have high energy and tend to be risk takers. It also suits them because they enjoy change, so business or sales jobs are great for them because they love the creativity. But this type of creativity is not measured well in school. Students, for the most part, are measured by the ability to retain and recall information. People who have high grade points are like computers, with the ability to store mass amounts of information in a neat and orderly manner and then recall it when needed. As I said before, this is simply a gift that is handed down from generation to generation and not necessarily from better study habits or higher levels of supposed intelligence.

I compare the brain to a computer for a reason. I think if you have a computer with all the parts working, you can work more effectively. If a part is broken or malfunctioning, then you cannot work at peak performance. The same goes for the brain, so for the fun of it, I will compare computer parts to how they might serve us in our lives if we had them in our brain:

- **Sound Card**: *You have the ability to be an effective communicator and verbally skillful.*

- **Video Card**: *You have great vision for the future and are creative in life and business.*

- **Processor**: *You can think problems through and process information quickly.*

- **Hard Drive**: *You have good long-term memory and store life lessons for future recall.*

- **RAM** *(Random Access Memory): This provides you with the ability to store and recall information quickly.*

Your brain (computer) works great if everything above is functioning properly, so you will more than likely do well in school, which will provide you with a high GPA. However, in the case of a person with ADD or ADHD, it is like your RAM is damaged and not working effectively. All the other components are working fine, but because one part of your brain (computer) is not functioning perfectly, it causes problems. If your RAM is not working properly, then it means you will have trouble storing information that you might need to recall for a test. If you cannot recall the information quickly, you do poorly on tests and end up with a low GPA. Then the school system labels you with a GPA that you carry with you for the rest of your life. So even though the rest of your brain (computer) is working great, and you can still function at a very high level in most areas of your personal and business life, the stigma of the low grade point (from defective RAM) destroys your confidence and self-worth.

This all leads up to what my Gremlin is and how it came to be. I was asked to do a vocational report in my eighth-grade English class, with the intent of helping us identify our career goals and prepare us for college with the right high school classes. I decided I wanted to be an Optometrist, because in my mind, I could be a doctor, avoid the trauma of blood and guts that regular doctors have to deal with, and make good money. I interviewed an Optometrist in town, and he showed me how everything worked. It was everything I dreamed of, and I was very excited about my newly chosen career. I did additional reading and research in order to make sure no stone was left unturned. I can tell you that it was some of the best work I had done in school, and it was a report that I was truly proud of.

I turned my report in and the English teacher rewarded me with a great grade, so I was very satisfied and encouraged by finally having a direction to follow when I graduated from high school. Knowing that this was my chosen career path, I took the report to my school counselor, so we could begin planning my high school classes around my college needs for optometry. I remember my counselor looking at the vocational report and thinking hard to herself as she paused. Then she said with caution, "*Brad, you might want to consider another profession because your grades aren't good enough.*" From my recollection, she continued talking about how there was a lot of math and science required, which were not my strong suits. I was somewhat in shock at her response, since I had my hopes so high for this profession, and I just stopped listening to her. My new found and well researched career had just been blown to bits.

Even though she was not mean spirited and was probably trying to protect me from the possibility of emotional pain or failure in college, the words I heard and focused on were *"not good enough."* My Gremlin was born that day, and it decided it was now responsible for reminding me on a regular basis that I was not good enough. My Gremlin did not have to look hard for opportunities to remind me that I was *"not good enough"* because my low grades alone continued to give it adequate ammunition.

How did it impact my behavior in school? I only went to one official high school sponsored dance because I was afraid to ask any girl to go with me because the Gremlin would whisper in my ear, *"You're not good enough."* The only dance I did attend was because a girl asked me out, for which I was thankful, because I did not have the courage to ask anyone. I never had a girlfriend in school, and I never really dated anyone officially. It was safer to just have girls that were friends because there was no emotional threat to my self-worth involved. My Gremlin would control me by trying to instill fear in me, and it was the fear of failure, rejection, humiliation and embarrassment. As we discussed earlier, fear is simply the anticipation of pain, so more than likely, I was never at risk of emotional pain, but when you are being told that you are not good enough by your inner voice, it leaves you uncertain and uncertainty kills dreams.

I look back on my life and realize that I was very competitive in many things. I competed in drag racing, karate, freestyle aerials, freestyle mogul skiing, ballet skiing, golf, tennis, water skiing and many other activities. Do you know why I competed in everything? It was so I could see if I was *"good enough."* I beat myself up and pounded my body over a 30-year period trying to prove to myself that I was good enough. No one else questioned whether I was good enough, so it was not about proving it to anyone else; I was simply trying to prove it to myself. My parents certainly felt I was good enough, my sister thought I was good enough, my friends thought I was good enough, but yet it wasn't enough because this little voice in my ear kept reminding me of that day back in eighth grade when I selectively gleaned the words *"not good enough"* from a conversation with my counselor, and my grades continued to reinforce that she must be right. The inner saboteur has kept those haunting words in front of me my entire life.

I am fortunate because I discovered my Gremlin at the age of 46, so I can hear and identify its disempowering language now. It still tries to convince me that I am not good enough, but I hear it, and I have learned to manage it. As I said before, if you don't manage it, it will continue to manage you because it will be with you the rest of your life – it is not going away. It is interesting that I hear my Gremlin about six or eight times a day, but the question is: how often is it speaking to me and trying to control me and I don't hear it? It might be 15 or 20 times a day, and it still might be winning the war, so I am not finished with trying to create more awareness about my Gremlin – it is a work in progress. I truly believe that more awareness will bring more change.

I hear my Gremlin speak when I am making sales calls to company executives. The Gremlin whispers in my ear and tries to keep me from making the call by reminding me that I am *"not good enough"* to talk to important people. They probably don't have time for me, and they will probably tell me so, or they will tell me "No" if I ask for an appointment. My Gremlin tried to stop me from writing each of my three books and most of my training videos by threatening me with *"But what if no one buys them"* and other disempowering words. It even delayed me from performing the seminar on this exact same subject for more than six years because it would whisper, *"But what if no one likes it"* and *"You're a customer service and leadership expert, not a motivational speaker, so no one will listen."* I finally realized the self-doubt in my head was not based on quantifiable facts or realistic research; it was simply the Gremlin doing what it does best, trying to scare me into conformity and keep me from taking risk and trying new things.

The most powerful thing I can tell you about your Gremlin is that it lies.

THE GREMLIN'S STORY IS NOT TRUE!

It creates fictitious stories that are absolutely not true, and they are intended to deceive and manipulate you. Even though its words are untrue, we still develop loyalty to them because the voice is relentless, and we begin to have self-doubt. Since I was about 14 years old, the Gremlin has been trying to convince me that I am not good enough based on an isolated moment in time. Out of an entire conversation with my school counselor, it chose three words to capture and remind me of constantly: *"not good enough."* The silly part is that my counselor was talking about my grades and not me, so how on earth could I develop loyalty to a story that is not true? And my grades are not who I am, they are what I had in school and they do not define me or how successful I can be in life. The same thing with being ADD; it is not who I am, it is what I have. ADD does not define me as a person; it is simply a learning challenge I have, which I have the ability to overcome (and did) I even look at my ADD as a blessing because I believe it is the reason that I am a great entrepreneur and successful business person who is not afraid of change and to take risks. I know many extremely successful people who are ADD or ADHD and they too have learned that it can be a gift and not a curse, even though it did not serve them well in school.

A great example of how the Gremlin can blatantly lie in the face of overwhelming evidence to the contrary is anorexia. How is it that an 18-year-old girl, who weighs only 75 pounds, can look in the mirror and see herself as fat? How can that story in her head be so powerful that it can overlook the obvious, which is that she is 40 pounds below her normal body weight? Yet the little voice in her head has convinced her that she is overweight and must stop eating.

The doctor can tell her that she is 40 pounds under weight, the scale can quantify to her that she is 40 pounds under her normal weight, but she looks in the mirror, and the inner voice, the saboteur, can convince her that she is looking at a fat person.

The Gremlin is a master manipulator, and it knows how to play you. One of the bigger challenges is that it performs its Satanic duties below our radar screen at a subconscious level, so it goes undetected. Its voice goes undetected because it has become a part of our daily dialogue of self-doubt. When we do hear its voice, we mistakenly believe that it is our ally or friend and that it is trying to serve us by protecting us from emotional pain. It delivers stories of potential fear on the horizon in hopes of getting us to back down from change and revert back to conformity. However, it is change that helps us achieve our greatest desires, so your Gremlin is the primary saboteur for your attempts at living an extraordinary life and achieving your greatest desires.

Even though you only have one Gremlin, it has a collection of emotional wounds of which to remind us. Even though our Gremlin is normally born through an emotionally traumatic event from our school years, we pick up many additional wounds throughout life, which unfortunately gives our Gremlin extra ammunition with which to control us and scare us back into conformity. They are, however, related and most revolve around our self-worth and self-image.

Imagine you are well beyond your school years and dating a fabulous person who you hope to marry some day. They are charming, fun, love all the same activities that you do, and their family is great as well. You have conversations about your future as you talk about how many kids you want, where you want to live, what kinds of animals you will own, and it just seems like a perfect fit. Then one day, you find out that they have been cheating on you with someone else – you are crushed. The relationship is now over, but the emotional wound is far from over. The Gremlin will grab onto that wound and remind you of the heartbreak every time you date someone new.

Each time a new person starts to seem like the perfect mate; your Gremlin will whisper in your ear, *"Sure, this one seems perfect – just like the last one that cheated on you!"* Each time you start to feel love, you begin to sabotage the relationship in order to protect yourself from the potential of emotional pain. You killed each relationship, and for what? To protect yourself? Seems odd, but that is what we do to ourselves with the help of our buddy, the Gremlin.

Let us say that you have worked for the same company for 10 years, and your direct supervisor is about ready to retire. You have done all of his duties at some point, so you fully understand his responsibilities and you know you could perform them. You also have a good working relationship with his peers and the other employees in your department. There is absolutely no reason that you should not apply for your supervisor's job when it gets posted. You notify your friends, family and co-workers that you are going to apply for this job and you are sure you have it in the bag. The day comes, so you apply for the job with complete confidence. The company president calls you into his office a couple weeks later when they are ready to announce who got the job. You walk in the office prepared with your acceptance speech and then find out that they hired someone from outside the company. Now, every time a position opens up for a promotion, your Gremlin pops up and says, *"Do you remember the last time you applied for a promotion? Do you remember the rejection and how embarrassing that felt?"* You freeze yourself in time, afraid to seek a better future for yourself because of one isolated circumstance that might have had nothing to do with your abilities. The uncertainty about yourself or someone else's decision killed your dreams and desires.

I have known a couple of people in my life that were both given up by their parents at a young age and adopted by great families who were loving and generous. I noticed something similar about both of these people (who did not know each other), and it was that they struggled with falling in love. They would not allow themselves to fall in love because their Gremlins were trying to protect them from the potential pain of rejection. From their perspective, they both had birth parents who "rejected" them by giving them up for adoption. It doesn't make any difference what the story surrounding their adoption was because that is irrelevant in their minds; it is the fact that someone who they loved and supposedly loved them, gave them up. I watched them sabotage relationship after relationship because their Gremlins were trying to protect them from ever being rejected again. Their thoughts were, *"If I fall in love with you, you might leave me."*

So how often do we sabotage ourselves, our dreams, our desires, our loves because of our Gremlin? The emotional wounds that the Gremlin likes to remind you of are not going away; they will be with you the rest of your life. The best you can hope for is to become aware of the Gremlin and the emotional wounds, so you have the ability to manage them. Unless you take control and begin to manage them, they will continue to control and manage you. One important aspect of being able to recognize the Gremlin's voice is to develop an awareness of it. If you find yourself in a situation where you are taking some risk but you hear a voice trying to talk you out of it, write it down. Ask yourself the question: is the voice in my head the voice of reasoning, and is it presenting me with quantifiable facts (facts and statistics that can be measured and validated) or is it the Gremlin's voice, which is simply a story created to generate fear in me? Keep a list of the Gremlin's words, and you will begin to see a pattern of how it is trying to scare you into conformity. You will see a pattern of threats and words that are focused on a previous wound, your self-worth or your self-image. Taking control of the Gremlin can occur if you learn to hear its voice and the words that it uses.

Let's talk about how we can take control of our Gremlin. Understanding and realizing the self-talk of the inner saboteur is the most critical part of taking control of your life. The Gremlin is the narrator in your head, and it wants you to accept its script as reality. Taking control of the Gremlin is a matter of becoming very clear about who you are and realizing that the stories it creates are simply myths. List the negative self-talk that drains you of energy, freezes you in time, and talks you out of trying new things or from taking risks (the Gremlin's script):

- _____
- _____
- _____
- _____
- _____
- _____
- _____
-

Now, make a list of your strengths, your successes, the things that give you energy, make you happy, make you feel powerful and allow you to see opportunity (the truths about you):

- _____
- _____
- _____
- _____
- _____
- _____
- _____
- _____

Re-write the script in your head about who you are and imagine the powerful new you. It should be one or two sentences long; short and sweet – right to the point. Don't write about who you "want" to become, because that is about "someday" (which is like the eighth day of the week that never comes); write about who you are right now. It is OK to feel powerful about you. It is OK to feel good about you. This is not an exercise in ego; it is an exercise about defining who you truly are. There should be no guilt or apologies about writing great things about you. Guilt does not serve you because it is a Gremlin emotion. This is an exercise in authenticity, and it is important to live each day as the true you because if you do not, you tend to draw the wrong people and results into your life. Start out your new script with the words "I am........." (i.e., I am powerful and smart, so there is nothing I cannot do. etc.).

_____

_____

_____

_____

If you chose not to complete the exercises, ask yourself why you did not do them. Is this your life? Do you try to take shortcuts in life, or are you too lazy to do the work? How has that worked for you? Do you try to do as little work on yourself as possible and how has that served you? Remember the old saying, "*If you continue to do the things you have always done, you will continue to have the things you have always had*" and for some of you, that is very little. Or, is your Gremlin trying to talk you out of it? If there is an inner voice trying to convince you that you don't have time for the exercises, or you don't need it, or you did it in your head, which is good enough, then your Gremlin is in complete control of you, and it will continue to be. It loves the fact that it can talk you out of deepening your learning and making positive changes in your life because it hates change. The Gremlin will continue to control you unless you go back now and do the work required to take control of it. The harder it is fighting you right now, the more you need to go back and do the work; otherwise, you might as well stop reading the book at this point because the rest will do you no good.

As I have said before, no thought lives rent free in your head, so we truly do create our own limits. The good news is we have the ability to rewrite the script and change our limits, so they turn into action. In my seminar, I ask for a volunteer to come to the front of the room and stand facing the front. I place a laser pointer in their hands (the kind just like you torture your cats with as you have them chase the red dot on the floor or wall). I ask them to place their feet about shoulder width apart and then point both arms straight out in front of them with both hands holding the pointer, having it point at the wall in front of them. Then I ask them to turn to the left as far as they can, as everyone in the room watches the laser light move across the wall. When they stop, I have another volunteer place a sticky note on the wall at the exact place the laser pointer ended up (it marks how far they could turn their body to the left). I ask the person holding the laser light, to look at the sticky note very carefully and remember where they ended up. Then I ask them to stand facing the front of the room again, just like before, but close their eyes this time and imagine doing the same exercise again, but going six feet past their previous spot. Once they have imagined it, they turn to the left again with their eyes open, and they are always able to move past the original place with the sticky note by at least six feet or more. The other volunteer marks the spot on the wall again with another sticky note, and I ask the person with the laser pointer to do the process once again and go six feet beyond their last mark. Yes, they always go past it by at least six feet and most of the time more.

After they complete that exercise, I ask them why they did not go to the third sticky note the first time. My request was very clear:

"Turn to the left and go as far as you can." The only answer that ever comes up is that they went as far as they thought they could go the first time. Then, when challenged with a new goal to achieve, they pushed themselves to attain it. Then when challenged again with a new goal, they pushed themselves again even further to attain it. This is the way most people function each and every day of the week, month and year: we go as far as we <u>think</u> we can, not as far as we are capable of. We set our own standards and rarely push ourselves to achieve anything greater (we do only what is comfortable, not what is truly attainable). This is one of the reasons that setting goals for ourselves, our children, and our employees is very important. If we don't set very specific goals that sometimes push us a little, we will only do what is comfortable and that will rarely lead us to an extraordinary life or help us achieve our greatest desires.

If the script in your head is:

- *"I will never get out of debt," then you probably won't*
- *"I don't think I will ever find true love," then you probably won't*
- *"I will never be the president of a company," then you probably won't*
- *"I can never see myself making $250,000 per year," then you probably won't*
- *"I will never be able to afford to own my own home," then you probably won't*
- *"I can't imagine what it would be like to own a yacht," then you probably won't*

Don't go after what you think you are qualified for; go after what you truly want. Don't go as far as you think you are capable of going, like in the exercise above; go as far as you need to go in order to have the things that you want in life – push yourself to new limits. The script in your head (and everyone has one) is real, and it will help determine your future, so take the time (a lot of time if needed) and carefully craft the script for your life. Make it powerful and make it big. If you get nervous about writing it down and committing to it-GREAT! That means the Gremlin is scared because it sees you wanting to change and wanting to grow, and it hates change. If you are scared about your script, it means you are moving into new territory and a new life, which is exactly the reason you are reading this book – one filled with unlimited possibility and opportunity.

It will take time to replace your old script with your new one, so it is crucial that you look at your new script before you begin every single day for at least 90 days. Take a copy of your new script and place it on your bathroom mirror, so you see it every day. Re-read it a couple of times each day until you have memorized it and you begin to live and breathe those words. Maybe also program the electronic calendar in your computer or cell phone to have your new script pop up around noon, every day for the next 90 days, to help remind you of the new you. You need to drive it from a conscious place to a subconscious place in your brain, so it becomes a behavior habit that drives new thoughts, feelings and actions.

Earlier in this chapter, we talked about the Reticular Activating System being a filter and how it takes instructions from your conscious mind and passes them on to your subconscious. It helps transfer conscious thought into subconscious thought where it becomes an automated response, which is where you need your new script to be. With a little diligence, you can use your Reticular Activating System to become your ally and filter only positive affirmations about your-self instead of the current negative ones that your Gremlin created (which are lies). You can use it to re-program your brain for your new script; set goals and help you visualize an extraordinary life and achieve your greatest desires. It can help you filter out negative responses and stimuli heading for your brain and shut them down. Your Reticular Activating System cannot distinguish between what is real and what is made up, so whatever you give it, it will send on down to your subconscious. Remember, if you believe you cannot live an extraordinary life or achieve your greatest desires, your subconscious can be programmed for that as well, which is the way many of you are programmed right now. It may just be the Gremlin's stories and lies, but the Reticular Activating System has no way of knowing that, so it sends it on down to the subconscious, and that becomes the new automated response that controls your every move.

Knowing how your brain works and how your conscious thoughts can become your subconscious automated responses, is critical to your successful transformation. Because you are reading this book, you now possess knowledge that 99.9 percent of the population does not so think of the opportunities that lie ahead for you and don't lie ahead for others. Now, for the first time ever, you have an opportunity to have an extraordinary career and life, and achieve your greatest desires. Congratulations, you are one step closer!

Chapter 7

ARE YOU SOARING WITH EAGLES OR HANGING WITH TURKEYS?

I truly believe that you cannot soar like an eagle and achieve your greatest desires if you hang with turkeys. The people that surround you, especially your peers, can mold who you are and who you end up being by their influence on you. Their influence will be subtle, and your brain will not recognize their words as a danger sign that your future is in jeopardy. Your friends' influence often happens at your subconscious level below your awareness, so you do not recognize that their words or actions are bad for you. In short, some of the people you associate with can become your Gremlin because they will try to keep you the way you are.

Your friends may fear (fear = the anticipation of pain) that if you go to college and get a degree, go to a trade school for specialized training, join the Army and learn a marketable skill, or even go to a seminar that empowers you, that you might become successful, and they may not. If you move forward and become successful and they do not, it may make them look bad and that may terrify some of the people currently in your life. Their fears will drive them to talk you out of your dreams or desires. They will do the same thing as the

Gremlin and try to sabotage you by instilling fear, scaring you into conformity and causing you to back down from trying new things.

They may use Gremlin language such as, *"But what if you fail in college and don't get your degree?"* or *"What if you spend all that money on school and you can't find a job?"* They also might be more direct and get in your face with threatening Gremlin language such as, *"You're not ready,"* *"You're not smart enough,"* *"You're not good enough,"* or *"You will never pull it off."* As their level of fear goes up, so does their need to talk you out of your personal growth and desires. Remember, Gremlins will mask themselves as friends or allies, so you will think they are trying to protect you. However, these friends are self-serving because they are only trying to protect themselves from the emotional pain of failure, rejection, humiliation or embarrassment.

As an example of how people close to you can become your Gremlin without you realizing it. I have been volunteering weekly with a domestic violence organization in our community since 2003. Abusers (primarily men who physically, sexually or emotionally abuse women) are the victims' real life Gremlin, and they try to isolate victims from their family and friends with their lies. Then they try to convince the victims that no one else would love them because they are not pretty enough, not smart enough, or not good enough (Gremlin language). They control and dominate the victims by instilling fear into them, just like any other Gremlin. They become that inner voice that acts like an advocate because they tell them how much they love and care for them and how they are their only true friend but then abuse them at will and try to convince the victims afterwards that the abuse was their fault (i.e. *"I would not have to hit you if you weren't so stupid."*) Abusers are the worst kind of Gremlins because they are real, dangerous, and they will not go away easily. Even when the abuser is finally removed from their lives, people who have been abused will have to live with that emotional trauma for the rest of their lives. All of the words that the abuser (Gremlin) used were lies, but those words will stick with them, just as the words *"You're not good enough"* have stuck with me all these years. Abuse is an emotional wound that the inner voice (Gremlin) will never allow the victim to forget and will remind them of that wound for the rest of their lives.

Why would people who supposedly care about you continue to remind you of your imperfections or weaknesses? Why would they work so hard at trying to keep you in a controlled state of fear, incapable of moving forward toward an extraordinary life? This is the reason it is hard for many young people to move from where they are to where they want to be. It is the peer pressure that is holding them back because they don't have the strength to fight their Gremlins. This can occur in any country, providence, state, city, village, tribe or cul-de-sac in the world where kids may be struggling with their own self-worth. They may already be dealing with challenging influences from their environment or culture and with peers who might not want to see them succeed because they don't want to get left behind. I call these people Energy Vampires because they are trying to suck the life out of you, in order to control you and keep you small.

Life is full of Energy Givers and Energy Vampires. We have talked about how Energy Vampires can drain us of energy and try to keep us small. These people can be friends or family members. Family members who are Energy Vampires are the worst because they are supposed to love us and be supportive of us. Our family is supposed to be faithful to us and have our back at all times, but some of them unfortunately can have the same fears as our Energy Vampire friends. They may fear being left behind or they might fear that you will become successful, which may be something they never achieved in their life, and it could make them look bad.

It might even be a parent who made bad life choices and never made anything of themselves or tried and failed, then gave up. It might be a parent who plays the victim role and instilled into you that *"the man has held us down"* or that *"we don't have a chance for a future because our people are discriminated against"* or *"the rich get richer and the poor get poorer, so we don't have a chance."* Victims will look back into the past and try to find someplace in time where there was a wrong done to them or their people and replay that story in their head. Worse yet, they will share it with their children until it becomes the script replayed in their children's heads as well. This is a place where prejudice breeds and becomes a cancer that kills dreams, desires and lives.

I am not trying to minimize the wrongs that have occurred in our past history because there are thousands of books on the subject. How could Native Americans have been treated so poorly over the years since settlers arrived on this continent? There is the unforgivable injustice of capturing and enslaving Africans, and how on earth could Hitler have killed millions of Jews and justify it to anyone? Even during World War II, when the United States went to war against Japan, the military gathered up Americans of Japanese heritage and interned them until the war was over, even though they had nothing to do with it. All of these events (and many more) in history are real, hard to understand, hard to explain and can breed victimization in some people.

If you want to find wrongs from the past, you don't have to look that far. Even though no one should ever forget the past, how does it serve us when we use the past to poison someone's future? It is like drinking poison and hoping someone else dies. It doesn't serve you to punish people today for the sins of the past. Education and enlightenment about the past is a good thing because for many people, it represents their heritage, which should be embraced. However, as you speak to your children, I would encourage you to ask yourself the question: is what I am going to say education and enlightenment, or is it going to spread fear and hatred in the child? Please just give consideration to the message and how it will serve them in life. You want your children and grandchildren to have extraordinary careers and lives, and achieve their greatest desires, so ask yourself, does my story serve them in their future or victimize them and perpetuate the story to their detriment?

Chapter 7: ARE YOU SOARING WITH EAGLES
OR HANGING WITH TURKEYS?

93

Our stories can become other people's reality that can shape their destiny. For example, say that you are going on a hike in the Olympic Mountains in Washington State and a friend of yours, who hikes in that area a lot, tells you to be careful because there are rattlesnakes everywhere along the trail. About a mile into your hike, the tall grass along the trail rustles, and your body reacts with a rush of adrenaline, increased blood flow and heavy breathing. Based on what you were told, your perception becomes your reality, and you run back to your car to escape this venomous monster who nearly took your life. When you get home, your story is one of being attacked by a rattlesnake and barely getting away with your life. The reality is, there are no rattlesnakes in the Olympic Mountains, and your friend was just trying to have fun with you. Your nervous system is incapable of distinguishing between actual or imaginary fear; it responds the same way to either one.

How often, based on what someone tells us, does our perception become our reality and impact our mind and body? It doesn't make any difference if it is the truth or not because it simply becomes our reality and the story replayed in our head. If we are told that poverty is the best we can expect, does our mind and body react and does it create that as our reality? If we are told that we are not good enough, or that we are not smart enough, or that *"our people are repressed,"* could that become our reality because we believe it to be true? Do we sometimes set our own limitations based on what we are told, and do they shape our future? Absolutely! So if we imagine that we are successful and powerful, does our mind and body react to that and create our reality? Absolutely!

For about 22 years, I had wanted to own a large powerboat (about 47 feet), and it sat on my wish list of things that I wanted to achieve in my life. However, I never truly believed I would own one because I was raised in a small logging town, and that is not something anyone around me had as I was growing up. In spite of that, I felt it did not hurt to keep it on my list just in case I won the lottery and found myself with tons of extra money. At the age of 54, I finally decided that it was the "Most important" thing to me. Fortunately, I was surrounded with people who convinced me that I was capable of owning something so great. I went to sleep every night for months dreaming about untying the boat, pulling away from the dock, navigating the boat around Lake Washington with my family and friends, and I could actually feel the joy of the experience. It felt so real to me because I could even feel the adrenaline rush from certain moments

Your perception about yourself becomes your reality

and my heart race when I brought the boat back into my imaginary slip after each outing. My mind and body reacted so that it no longer seemed like it was meant for the future; it was meant for now. I actually convinced myself that I was worthy of such an adventure, and when I finally bought it, I felt like I had owned and driven it before because of how vivid my dreams were. In short, owning the boat became a reality because the beliefs and support of my loved ones helped me re-shape my self-image.

Without a good support group around you and a community of advocates who have your back, it is easy to buy into the Gremlin's story. If you buy into the fictitious stories in your head, and you don't have anyone around to shake you back into reality, it can make you feel isolated from the world and dig you into an even deeper emotional hole. Your perception about yourself becomes your reality, and your negative self image stays etched in stone because you don't have anyone around you to break the image.

Thank goodness that the world is abundant in Energy Givers, such as the ones in my life. These are people who give us energy and make us feel good about us and the world around us. They might be friends who are supportive of our ideas and are willing to jump in and help if needed. When you tell them that you have a great idea for a new company, they listen with sincere interest and will tell you the truth because it serves you best. You might want to ask your

Chapter 7: ARE YOU SOARING WITH EAGLES
OR HANGING WITH TURKEYS?

95

supervisor for the promotion that you have always wanted, and your friends applaud your desires and encourage you to go for it!

If you become successful, Energy Givers don't abandon you because *"you have changed;"* they embrace your good fortune and continue to serve as a friend. Their own self-worth is strong enough to handle someone else being successful, because in life, there will always be someone with more wealth or more stuff than you. Someone else's success should not threaten or intimidate you because that is about them and not you. If you try to make it about you and why you don't have what they have, then that is your Gremlin at work trying to drain you of energy by making you question yourself and your own self-worth. The Gremlin is great at trying to beat you up, and it will look for any opportunity to find what is wrong with you and hold it up to your face and rub it in. That is how it controls and manipulates you, by reminding you of your imperfections and reminding you of what you are not, or what you do not have. It will torture you with your primal fears of not being good enough or not having enough.

I truly believe that associating with successful people helps you raise your personal bar and nudges you closer to your own greatness (whatever greatness means to you). For those of you who are golfers, you already know that when you play with people who are poor golfers, you probably play your normal game and get your normal score (or you might even play below your normal game because you don't have to be at the top of your game to win). However, when you play with someone who is better than you, it seems to kick your game up a notch and pushes you to higher scores than you previously thought you were capable of. I have seen this true in car racing, water skiing, tennis and most other competitive sports. Our daily life is no different, and if we associate with people who we respect and represent success for us (once again, success is different for everyone), we have a greater opportunity to achieve it ourselves. Success becomes real when we can see what it looks like and know that it is attainable since it is all around us. It helps us re-frame negative self-talk from "*I can't*" to "*I can*" and motivates you to greatness.

I would like to offer you an exercise that might help you develop clarity around who serves you in life and who is holding you back. This can be difficult for many of you because you may really enjoy your Energy Vampire friends. You may try to talk yourself out of listing them as Energy Vampires because there are certain times when they are good for you and certain times when they are bad. You need to know that great friends are loyal to you and your mental health all the time.

Associate with people who are supportive of the true you; people that give you energy plus reinforce and support your positive attributes all the time. There are no "days off" from being a good friend and no excuses for not being supportive. Remove people from your life who drain you of energy, those who are negative and non-supportive. Make a list below of the people who you perceive as Energy Givers and Energy Vampires. Review your list and don't make excuses for them.

Energy Givers	**Energy Vampires**

Chapter 7: ARE YOU SOARING WITH EAGLES
OR HANGING WITH TURKEYS?

97

**You have three choices in dealing with your Energy Vampires.
You can either:**

1. *Choose to salvage the friendship by asking them to change.*

2. *Reduce the amount of exposure to these people.*

3. *Eliminate them from your life completely.*

If you are going to ask them to change, you will want to choose
your words very carefully because your goal should be to seek solutions to your issues with them, not to seek blame or retaliation. If
you truly want to find solutions, you need to focus on what behavior
you want them to change. In other words, make sure your words are
focused on the "issue" and not them personally because you do not
want your conversation to feel like a personal attack.

I will offer you ten tips on how to have a constructive conversation; however, it does not guarantee success because it will certainly
depend on the individual you are having this conversation with,
their emotional resiliency and their desire to want to change. Your
responsibility is the truth, as long as it is delivered in a responsible
manner. How they handle the truth is their responsibility. Here are
the ten steps that will help you have a good constructive conversation
with a better chance of a positive outcome:

1. *Make sure they have adequate time and that you are in an
   appropriate setting.*

2. *Ask permission before beginning your conversation.*

3. *Start off by offering a sincere compliment to them.*

4. *Talk about the "issue" that you want to resolve and not "them."*

5. *Make your feedback specific and targeted – not vague.*

6. *Avoid gang up language like "We all think" or "Many people
   believe."*

7. *Use "I" and "We" to stress that you want to work out the
   issue together.*

8. *Don't belabor the point; make it short and sweet with no lectures.*

9. *Don't set a tone of anger or sarcasm and do not have the conversation when angry.*

10. *At the end, reaffirm your support and confidence in the person.*

Step 1: You want to make sure to have this conversation in a quiet place where they can hear you properly and where there are no distractions. This type of conversation may be traumatic for some people, so it is best to have it away from other people, so there is no risk of embarrassment. You also want to make sure that they have adequate time to have the conversation because you do not want to have to be watching the clock during this type of interaction. Out of respect, you do not want the conversation to be rushed or have to end abruptly without making it to Step 10.

Step 2: You also want to avoid offering advice or asking someone for a favor (like for them to change) unless you have been invited in to do so. I would suggest you start the conversation by saying something like *"Can we talk about our friendship?"* or *"Would it be OK with you if we talked about the disagreement we had yesterday?"* You will then wait for the person to answer with a *"Yes"* or *"No."* If they answer with a *"Yes,"* then you can move right to Step 3. If they respond with a *"No,"* I would suggest you ask *"Why?"* To me, this response would signal that there truly is a deeper problem, and they do not want to go through the effort to resolve it or they may simply want to avoid drama. However, this is more than likely a pattern for this person and one of the reasons that they may not make a good friend to you.

Step 3: Since they have been a friend, there must be something that you enjoy about them (an endearing quality detached from the issue), and this is the time to let them know about the characteristic that you enjoy. You want them to know there are reasons that you enjoy their friendship, so let them know what behaviors or attributes you respect or admire. I have always believed that praise breeds change,

Chapter 7: ARE YOU SOARING WITH EAGLES
OR HANGING WITH TURKEYS?

99

so by praising them on their positive attributes, they might choose to do more of them and avoid the detracting attributes that make them an Energy Vampire (in your eyes). A few kind words can also help reduce their anxiety and keep them from being confrontational.

Step 4: I would suggest that you rehearse the words you want to use and pick them carefully, so they are focused on the issue, not the person, in order to avoid the conversation feeling like a personal attack. In other words, if your issue is that they are always late to meet you, focus on "being late" as the issue. The focus should be on your perception and how it makes you feel. No one should be able to challenge you about your perceptions or feelings because they are YOURS, not anybody else's. If you quote someone else's opinion, then they could become arguable, but your feelings are what they are – yours! As an example, you might say, "*Last week you asked me to meet you on Monday, Wednesday and Friday at noon for lunch and you arrived 30 minutes late all three days. When you are late for lunch, it also makes me late getting back from lunch to my job, which is getting me in trouble. My perception is that you don't value my time and that makes me feel undervalued as a friend.*"

Step 5: You can see in the above example, I used very specific dates and times to make my point because they are irrefutable (so make sure they are). If I would have said, "*You are always late*" or "*You never show up on time,*" that would invalidate my point because even though they may be late 90 percent of the time, that is not "all" the time. Anytime we use the words "always" or "never" to make our point, we can be accused of exaggerating or lying, which diverts the attention away from the issue that you want to resolve. They will stop listening to anything that comes out of your mouth after those two words because they perceive your conversation as inaccurate or exaggerated.

Step 6: Avoid using "gang up language" to make your point because it will only make matters worse. Trying to make the person feel like everyone feels the same way as you simply creates drama and redirects the conversation away from the issue again. As an example, you would never want to say, "*All of our friends feel the same way as I do about you being late*" or "*Everyone is as mad at you as I am.*" It only makes the person feel picked on or attacked and will put them on the defensive, which kills any possibility of a peaceful solution.

Step 7: If you use words such as "I" and "we" it will imply that you want to work out the issue together. It might be used like this: "*I truly want to have a great friendship with you, and I know we can make it stronger.*" You might even see if there is anything you can do to assist them with overcoming their issue, such as "*Is there anything that I can do to help resolve the issue?*" Their problem may be that the times you set to meet are unreasonable for their schedule or they may have some logical reason for why they are always late (logical reasons you can accept and help find a solution to, but excuses should not be acceptable).

Step 8: I don't know anyone who wants to feel lectured to or who wants to hear about the same issue over and over again. It is best to keep the conversation short, sweet and right to the point no matter how much you might want to re-emphasize the issue and keep drilling it into them. If you continue to drive your point and become repetitive, it might leave them with the perception that you think they aren't smart enough to get it the first time or that they don't care. As much as you may be tempted to continue your dialogue, it will not serve you well in the long run.

Step 9: I would encourage you to avoid these conversations when you are annoyed, angry, frustrated, irritated or emotionally charged in any way. The chances of remembering all of these steps or being able to carry them off gracefully is just not going to happen. You also want to avoid any tone of voice that might send the message that you are frustrated. This is also a good time to pay attention to your body language, which includes your facial expressions (avoid "stink eye," which sends a very clear message that you are angry). I can tell you that 100 percent of the letters or E-mails that I have written when I was emotionally charged, and let sit overnight, got re-written the next day to make them more respectful and effective – every single one of them.

Step 10: You want to avoid leaving anyone feeling wounded or hurt by your conversation, so this is a good time to reaffirm your friendship, support and confidence in the person. Let them know that you truly appreciate them taking time to talk about the issue and that you know things will be fine. Reconfirm the positive attributes about the person and have them walk away with their chin held high and a smile on their face.

Let's talk about another option available when dealing with Energy Vampires. That may be simply to change the amount or type of contact with them, which will reduce the amount of emotional recovery time you deal with each day, week or month. This can occur by simply reducing the amount of communication. One example would be if someone on your Energy Vampire list is a family member. I would rarely advocate that you eliminate them from your life, unless they are truly evil and their intent is to cause harm to you or others, but you can change the way you communicate with them. You may choose to simply communicate less; so instead of calling them weekly, you might choose every two weeks, which reduces your trauma by half. The other option is to change the way you communicate completely. As an example, if every time you call your grandmother she starts the conversation out with "*Well, it's nice to finally hear from you – have you been too busy to call your only grandmother?*" You might choose to switch your method of communication from telephone to E-mail or text where they cannot torture you with their manipulative voice inflection. This way you can have great conversations, and you won't have to deal with the manipulative voice tone, which is the main reason that calling is so painful.

Let's talk about the last option, which is to remove Energy Vampires completely from your life. I am not suggesting that you pick up the phone and call your Energy Vampires and let them know that they are on your list, so "Bye bye!" I am suggesting that you disconnect from these people in whatever way you can without leaving hurt feelings (if possible). This is not about punishing them or trying to make them feel bad about themselves. They already have their own Gremlin, so they don't need anyone else to help beat them up. You simply might stop calling them, because maybe you are the one who works hard at keeping the friendship alive anyway, so just stop and they may drift away over time. They may be people who you have been hanging out with daily, so maybe you cut back to weekly in an effort to begin the separation process. If they confront you about the separation, I am a fan of honesty, but you will want to find a way to *"step on their shoes without ruining their shine,"* which is not easy. This may be a situation where you go back a few pages and follow the ten steps to have a constructive conversation with them. They might choose to change to your liking in an effort to save the friendship, or they might make the decision that the friendship is not worth it and simply drift off into the sunset, which is just fine.

Now that you have taken care of your Energy Vampires, I would suggest you plan to spend more time with your Energy Givers. If you enjoy these people on your list and they truly give you energy, are supportive, and make you feel good about you, be intentional about creating more time for these people in your life. As odd as it may sound, pick up your calendar and schedule time with these people. Maybe even create rotating dinner parties with a group of them, so you meet at least once a month at a different couple's house. The monthly couple who hosts it can either do all the preparation and entertaining or you can make each event a pot-luck where everyone brings something to eliminate the burden on just one couple. Maybe you also schedule a monthly get together for events like bowling, karaoke, movie night, happy hour or whatever you enjoy. Unless you schedule these people into your life, it may never happen. As we have talked about before, do not let your life become accidental, create intention for each day, each week, each month and each year.

This one act alone, of scheduling time for your Energy Givers, could make an impact on the quality of your life.

Some of you might be challenged with another problem, which is a friend who is a part time Energy Giver and part time Energy Vampire. You enjoy their company some of the time, but other times their fangs show and the Vampire comes out in them. No one can make this decision for you, but you will want to give consideration to the rewards vs. consequences of this friendship. Is there enough value in the relationship to warrant your dealing with the Vampire side of this individual? Are they supportive more than they are drainers? How much emotional recovery time is needed after your interaction with this person? You might consider making a list with two columns: one where you can list all the ways that they give you energy and in the other column list the ways that they drain you of energy. This will allow you to make a logical and rational decision based on some quantifiable facts, instead of a decision based on emotion, which may not serve you well.

The other option with this type of friend is to have an honest conversation with them and discuss the energy they bring you and the "issues" that drain you of energy and see if they would be willing to make some adjustments. This, of course, depends on the relationship you have with them and their own emotional stability to have a constructive conversation without being hurt. If you plan such a conversation, go back a few pages and read the section again that provides ten steps to having such a conversation. You are the only one who can determine if this friendship is important enough to you to take some emotional risks and seek solutions.

The last challenge that needs to be addressed is if you have a friendship with a couple where one is an Energy Giver and the other is an Energy Vampire. I wish I could tell you that I have a ten-step process for how to solve this issue, but I do not. This situation is really tough for everyone involved, so I will be the last one to tell you that I have all the answers. My only suggestion is to weigh the rewards versus consequences of spending time with them as a couple. How much energy does that giver provide you compared to the amount of damage and emotional recovery time involved in hanging out with the Energy Vampire?

You might also try to minimize your exposure to the person who is the Energy Vampire of the couple by knowing more about them. If they get mean when they get drunk and ruin functions by their behavior, avoid events where heavy drinking is an issue or create events that are void of liquor. If you have a friend who gets tired easily towards the end of events and their lethargic behavior kills the party, find an energy drink they would like and always keep the pantry stocked with them. This is more about managing the process in order to minimize the negative effects of the Energy Vampire.

The only other option is to have an individual friendship with the Energy Giver of the couple and create events where couples are not required. You might choose to invite your Energy Giver friend to lunch once a week where the two of you can meet and talk. You might schedule events that are more individual oriented like going shopping at the mall, going to the movies or any event where a couple is not required. It is possible to carry these friendships out, but it will eventually lead to an invitation as a couple, and that is where you have to weigh the rewards versus negative consequences and make your decisions accordingly.

We have talked about friends as Energy Givers and Energy Vampires, but what does the perfect friend look like? I have repeatedly requested that you be more intentional about your life, and with that in mind, I have another request for you: I would like you to define who your perfect friend is and what attributes they possess. This an opportunity to stop making friend selection accidental, which normally does not create the best results, and find friends that are perfect for you (why should you accept any less?). I would like you to write a brief advertisement for the perfect friend by listing the attributes you are looking for. You might start the ad with something like this:

"I am looking for a friend who has a great sense of humor, is respectful of other people, loves to entertain and have people over for dinner, etc."

_____

_____

_____

_____

_____

_____

Does your ad truly describe the perfect best friend for you? It should! If you are not married or committed for life, then this is a chance to re-evaluate your choice and see what attributes are negotiable and which ones are non-negotiable. If you are already in a long-term relationship or marriage, then this may be a good exercise for the two of you to do and compare lists. This may be a chance for open and honest dialogue about what the two of you can do to accommodate each other in order to live an extraordinary life. At this point, since you are committed to this person, flexibility and the ability to want to change are very important in order to make the relationship last. With that said, the one thing you will learn toward the end of this book is that "We take ourselves wherever we go," and there are some attributes that will never go away. In this case, the best you can hope for is that your partner can manage and control them, which is very hard for most people.

I would like you to write a list of the non-negotiable attributes that you would never allow in a best friend. When I use the words non-negotiable, I truly mean that these are attributes that are deal breakers, and you are not open to discussion on. If a person you meet has any single one of these attributes, you will make the decision to walk away and not pursue the friendship. You might start your list with something like this: "*The things I will not accept in a friend are anger management problems, controllers, people who do not respect my time, smokers, addictive personalities, etc.*"

_____

_____

_____

_____

_____

_____

Most thought and daily decision-making is done at a subconscious level and not at a conscious level (it is done on cruise control). Our subconscious normally offers automated responses and relies on "the way it has always been done." Living an extraordinary life and achieving your greatest desires comes from living at a higher level of consciousness and decision making. It also comes when we create more intention in our lives and take ourselves off cruise control. Most people wake up each day and begin doing what they have always done each day. Their actions are performed without much thought, and this is what cruise control looks like. Living an extraordinary life requires change in many areas of our lives, which is not comfortable for any of us and even gives us anxiety at times. Having great friends or relationships should not be accidental, nor should any other parts of our lives for that matter. If you are not clear about who you want in your life, you may continue to attract the wrong people into your life. Take yourself off cruise control, follow the steps in this book, have an extraordinary career and life, and achieve your greatest desires.

Chapter 8

HOW TO SET S.M.A.R.T. GOALS

Many people don't get what they want because they don't know what they want. In order to live an extraordinary life and achieve your greatest desires, you must be intentional. If we determine that we have a strong desire (one that is "Most important" to us), and if we want it to become a reality, sometimes we need to set specific goals to help us achieve it. When setting personal or professional goals, make sure that they are S.M.A.R.T. or you might be setting yourself up for failure.

- *Specific*
- *Measurable*
- *Achievable*
- *Realistic*
- *Timed*

As an example, if I told you that I wanted to reduce my stress, would that be a S.M.A.R.T. goal? Of course not, and one of the reasons is because it is not specific enough. Stress is a big subject and can have many causes, so by simply saying you want to set a goal to reduce your stress; you might be setting yourself up for failure. It may also be hard to measure and difficult to achieve without being more specific, which can also make it unrealistic. There was also no timeframe attached to the goal. The real key to setting S.M.A.R.T. goals is what specifically, are you going to do to make your goals become a reality and when will they be achieved?

Let's try this again and make stress reduction a S.M.A.R.T. goal this time: The desk in my office is messy, which has me feeling disorganized and is therefore stressing me out. Let's say today is Monday, and my goal is to reduce my stress by cleaning and organizing my desk by 5 p.m. this Friday. Is that now a S.M.A.R.T. goal? Let's analyze it and see:

- *Specific – Yes, because it is isolated specifically to my desk.*

- *Measurable – Yes, because once I am done, I can see my desk is clean and organized.*

- *Achievable – Yes, because it is something that I can easily accomplish in the time allowed.*

- *Realistic – Yes, because it is a real and practical goal.*

- *Timed – Yes, because I set a very specific time-line to complete it by 5 p.m. Friday.*

Even though many of you might be good goal setters, which one of the above five criteria do you think most people fail to attach to their goals? If you guessed "Timed," you are right. Why do you think many people do not set a time frame for completing their goals? It is because they have a fear of failure, so they are trying to protect themselves from the emotional pain of failure. If you don't set a specific time and date for your goals, then you can't feel like a failure if you don't get it done on time. The problem with this is that you are not holding yourself accountable, and in the process, you set yourself up for failure because you may not attain your goals. Letting yourself off the hook is not a good thing. You must hold yourself to the highest standards if you want to live an extraordinary life and achieve your greatest desires. With that said, you certainly should make sure that the time frame you set for yourself is realistic and achievable. ALWAYS set a very specific date and time for your goals, and you will find that you will achieve them. Why? Because most people fear failure so much that if they set a specific date and time, they will achieve it because they do not want to fail. Setting S.M.A.R.T. goals will make you more productive and focused, which will actually reduce the chances of failure. Creating a specific time-frame creates commitment, accountability and also reduces procrastination. This builds confidence and the cycle of success begins!

Setting S.M.A.R.T. goals helps you create more intention for your personal and business life. It helps prevent your life from being accidental, which most people's lives are. Most people wake up each day and go straight into cruise control. Most people do the same things each day the way they have always done them with very little thought. Since most humans dislike change, we brush our teeth the same way each day, shower the same, dress in the same order, leave for work at the same time, drive the same route, do the job the same way, drive home the same route, eat and go to sleep at the same time. We are creatures of habit and most people greet each day the same way: "*I hope today is going to be a good day.*" Instead of hoping, why don't you plan for a great day by setting S.M.A.R.T. goals daily?

If you would like a new car, why would you tell yourself "some day" I will get one? Once again, someday is like the eighth day of the week that never comes. Be methodical and create a S.M.A.R.T. goal for yourself by putting a very specific plan in place to make your goal become a reality. It creates a blueprint for success. A S.M.A.R.T. goal is a true plan for achieving your desire for a new car. It gives meaning to each day and makes your goals become realistic. Once you achieve your S.M.A.R.T. goal, it builds your confidence and motivates you toward even greater goals, which helps you achieve your greatest desires. Remember, the main difference between the rich and poor is simply the amount of confidence they have. Do whatever you can to build your confidence, and the end result will be your greatest desires realized.

I find it funny that we begin methodically planning our two-week vacation six months in advance. Every single day is planned with surgical precision because we want to have an extraordinary time. We plan each step of the trip from the time we leave the door of the house until we arrive home again and everything in between. We plan the flight, the hotel, transportation, the meals, side trips, plus the people and things we want to see. We set specific dates and times for each leg of our journey and plan for an extraordinary time. So why is it that we will methodically plan a two-week vacation but the other 50 weeks of the year are a complete accident? Aren't the rest of our lives worth planning and giving more thought to? We want our vacations to be extraordinary (which is why we give them so much thought, effort and preparation), so if we want our entire life to be extraordinary as well, doesn't it make sense that it deserves the same time, attention and thought?

Once you set a goal for yourself, you need a plan of action, and that requires clarity. Give some thought as to how to answer each of the questions below before moving forward.

- *What is your S.M.A.R.T. goal?* _____

  _____

- *What is your level of desire?*_____

  _____

- *What is your emotional motivator?* _____

  _____

- *What obstacles stand in your way?* _____

  _____

  _____

  _____

Desire, in itself, is a useless emotional request without a specific plan of action. The plan of action should help you identify the following:

1.   **What** *specific steps are required to achieve your goal?*
2.   **Who** *is going to be responsible for performing each of the steps?*
3.   **When** *will each of the steps be completed?*

In order to help you determine the three phases above, you can use a technique called "Idea Mapping." It is a visual thinking tool that utilizes the entire brain by using color, key words, lines and images to connect ideas. The reason for using this technique is that it allows you to capture free-flowing thoughts without over-analyzing them. It utilizes the brain's ability to process information through association. Idea Mapping is a simple process that helps people (or organizations) create clarity, deepen learning, problem solve, improve productivity and most importantly, save time.

One of the challenges people have in planning anything is that most people are linear thinkers, so we normally pick up a tablet of lined paper and begin writing down our thoughts. The problem is, we spend way too much time trying to write everything down in a specific order. The act of trying to think about what comes first and what comes second inhibits us from creative thinking, and sometimes sidetracks us. You may have heard the phrase "Analysis causes paralysis." Well this is a good example of how over-thinking can lock our brain up sometimes and make it hard to move forward. We are so mentally locked up with what comes next that we cannot see beyond that point to other steps that are important as well.

Idea Mapping is normally done on a single page of paper (preferably a large flip chart), which helps you visually capture ideas in a non-linear manner. I use this technique when I am beginning the process of writing a new book or a new seminar. I also use it for strategic planning for my clients and for my own business. You can use it for homework assignments, projects, presentations, planning vacations, creating a new business, building a new home, designing an extraordinary life or most anything where planning is needed. I am only going to introduce you to the condensed version of Idea Mapping, but there are many books available on the subject that go much deeper than I will. There are also many different looks to Idea Mapping by using different shapes and colors, but I am going to show you the one style I use the most. I do use colored pens during the process to differentiate the "who, what and when" subjects, however I will be limited to black and white in the book.

The first step in Idea Mapping is to make sure you have done the previous work and developed a S.M.A.R.T. goal. The entire Idea Mapping process revolves around the S.M.A.R.T. goal, so make sure you have given it your due diligence. This is not the place for a shortcut. The next step is to draw a box in the middle of a clean white piece of paper big enough in which to write your S.M.A.R.T. goal. You can also use a flip chart or larger pieces of paper if you need a larger work space or if you are Idea Mapping with a group of people (as in a strategic planning session). In order to give you an example of the process, I will create a fictitious S.M.A.R.T. goal as if I had a retail clothing store chain. My S.M.A.R.T. goal will be to add one new store in Seattle by December 31, 2011 (the date would be a S.M.A.R.T. goal as of the writing of this book allowing myself one year).

*Add one new
store in Seattle
by
12 / 31 / 2011*

The next step is to draw four legs off each corner and these will become the required steps to make the goal become a reality. You simply ask yourself *"What steps are required in order for my goal to become a reality?"*

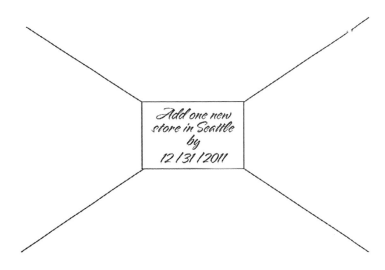

Add one new store in Seattle by 12/31/2011

Then you start writing the required steps on each of the four lines without consideration to which one is first or which one is last (the order is not important at this point). If you fill all four lines up with required steps, then you draw another empty line from the box wherever there is space (so you have a fifth line). You will see in an example coming up, where I created a fifth line that runs straight down from the middle of the box, but you can do it straight up or even to the sides. When I came up with another required step (in this example, marketing), I drew another empty line from the middle of the box straight up (so I now have a sixth line). The goal is to always have empty lines on the page because you want your brain to continue to seek answers. If your brain sees all the lines full, it will tend to believe it is done with its work and requires no further thought. It works harder when it perceives it is missing something.

If I had five of the lines filled in with 1) Find Location, 2) Arrange Financing, 3) Prepare Staffing, 4) Marketing and 5) Purchase Inventory, and the next idea to pop into my head was "Schedule Training," it would not be a new required step, it would be an action step under "Prepare Staffing," so I would draw a line off the required step "Prepare Staffing" and write in "Schedule Training" on the line. Any word, idea or step that pops into your head needs to be given consideration as to whether it is a "required step"(main requirement with a line off the goal box) or whether it is an "action step" (action required, whose line is drawn off the required step, to make the required step become a reality). There can also be "action steps" that are drawn off of "action steps" as shown below under the required step "Prepare Staffing." We have an action step called "Schedule Training," which we just talked about, and under that we have three other action steps that need to occur which are 1) Orientation, 2) Customer Service and 3) Leadership. In this example, the Idea Map shows that in order for the **new store to be open and operating by 12/31/11** (S.M.A.R.T. goal), we must **prepare our staff** (required step) in advance by **hiring employees** and **scheduling training** (two action steps), and we will need to provide them with **orientation, customer service and leadership training** (three action steps) in order to be successful. The same flow is true for each of the other steps on the Idea Map, and if they are all completed, it increases the potential for success. The only limits to how many steps there are is the size of your paper. If you run out of space, tape extra paper on to your sheet and keep going.

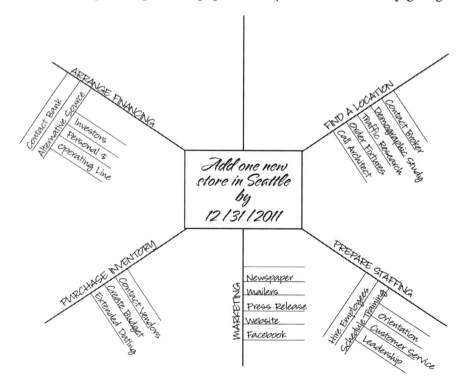

Idea Mapping provides an opportunity for the free flow of information without encumbering it with over-thought such as what particular order things have to be done in. This process should not be rushed, and if done properly, you might work for a few hours on it until you have no more ideas, take a break until the next day and come back to it again. You might even do as much as you can, then start again a few days later when you have had time to rest and process everything better. Once you have collected all the steps required to make your S.M.A.R.T. goal become a reality on the idea map, the next things you need to decide are:

- *Which steps get done first? (prioritize your required steps first, then action steps as well if you like)*
- *Who will perform each of the steps?*
- *What specific date each will each step be completed by?*

The end result can look pretty messy, but who cares? It is simply a working document. The idea is to end up with a plan that says "If each person completes all of their steps by the date assigned, we will make our S.M.A.R.T. goal become a reality."

If these are personal goals you are setting and you are the one doing all the steps, there is no need to write your name all over the map. However, you will still need to prioritize your steps and write specific dates next to each and stay true to your commitment. Whether your Idea Map is for personal or business goals, I would suggest moving these dates from the Idea Map over to your day timer or your computer calendar program and make sure you are always aware of impending dates. Here is what the final map may look like if you have a team working on the S.M.A.R.T. goal:

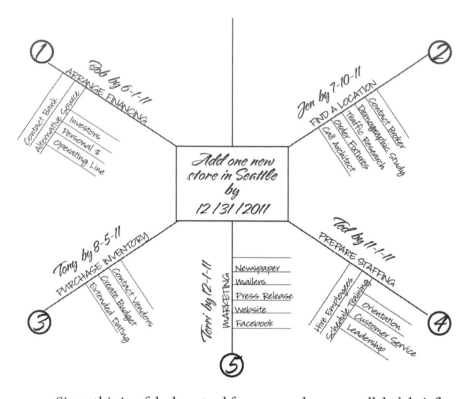

Since this is a fabulous tool for personal use as well, let's briefly look at what that may look like. If you are planning a vacation, this process works beautifully. The S.M.A.R.T. goal that you write in the box may be "two week trip to Paris on 1/6/2012." The required steps you write on the Idea Map may be: Money, Transportation, Lodging, Meals and Sightseeing. Under the required step "Money," you might have the following action steps: Save $200 per Paycheck, Open Money Market Fund, Track Exchange Rate and Take two Credit Cards. Under the required step of "Transportation," you might have the following action steps: Arrange Flight, Shuttle to Airport, Rent a Car and Rent Moped for One Day. You continue the process of writing all the action steps required for each of the required steps, then you prioritize the steps, determine who in the family will perform each of the steps and dates they will be completed. Before you know it, you are on the airplane heading off on an extraordinary trip without worry about what you may have forgotten. It is better to be proactive and enjoy your trip than to be reactive and have to put fires out during your two-week adventure.

In summary, setting S.M.A.R.T. goals and having a plan in place to make them become a reality is all about intent, commitment and accountability. This is the process of making a methodical, well-planned promise to yourself and following through on the commitment. If you have a friend who makes you a promise and does not follow through with it, it erodes their credibility with you. You learn not to trust them, and you might be prone to doubting their every word. If you make a promise to yourself and you break that promise, it can also erode your credibility in yourself. You begin to have self-doubt, and you begin to question your own capabilities. As we talked about in a previous chapter, one of the only differences between the rich and the poor is their level of confidence. You must be able to trust yourself, so stick to your plan because you cannot have an extraordinary career and life, and achieve your greatest desires if you have self-doubt.

Chapter 9
LANGUAGE THAT KEEPS US FROM GREATNESS

Many people have poor or disabling behavior habits that are tied to the words they use, and this is called disempowering language. Because habits are committed subconsciously and we give them very little thought, they are hard for us to be aware of. Habits are simply automated responses; they are not only very difficult to see or hear in ourselves, they are also very hard to stop. How can you stop doing something that you do not hear or see yourself doing? You also might not think that the words you use or the behaviors you exhibit have any negative meaning behind them, so there would be no reason to stop them. My goal in this chapter is to make you aware of some of the words you might be using and what the actual meaning behind them could be for you.

When you speak of your desires, goals, or action steps, do you use language that supports you? Sometimes our subconscious chooses words that sabotage our efforts such as:

- *"If.............."*
- *"I'll try........"*
- *"I wish........."*
- *"I hope........"*

- *"I can't........"*
- *"Someday...."*

As a personal example, I was using the word "*If*" quite a bit in my vocabulary without even knowing it. I would say "*If we get the boat*" or "*If I can get time off for a three-week vacation.*" This habit was brought to my attention by Melanie, and that really helped me develop an awareness of it. I truly believe that awareness can bring about change, so I was far more conscious of that word, and I began to drive it out of my vocabulary and replace it with the word "W*hen*," which is actionable. "*If*" sounds like it may or may not happen, which will never help you achieve your greatest desires, but when you say "*When,*" it is only a matter of time. This happened during a time when I really wanted a brand new 47-foot motor yacht (which I had wanted for 22 years), and when I also had the dream of a three-week vacation on the boat up into Canada. When I changed my "*If*" to a "*When,*" I had the boat within six months and the three-week vacation happened that summer. That shift of words can make your life more intentional and create internal commitment and accountability of which you might not even be consciously aware.

As another example, let's say you ask a friend if they want to meet you after work for a drink, and they respond with "***I'll try.***" Do you think they will show up? History shows that the words "*I'll try*" mean that they are not showing up, and the chances of you drinking alone are huge. As another example, if you asked one of your employees if they could have a report to you by Friday, and they walked away saying "*I'll try,*" do you think you will get the report? More than likely you won't.

The words "*I'll try*" are an escape route for some people, and even though their response is automated and not consciously derived, it has very deep meaning. These people have a fear of failure, so they avoid commitment, which also frees them from the accountability we talked about in the last chapter. You cannot live an extraordinary life and achieve your greatest desires without commitment and accountability. Remember, failure is the anticipation of pain. People who say *"I'll try"* are afraid to say "*Yes*" because that is a commitment or a personal promise to a specific timeline, and they do not want to be held that accountable. If they never say "*Yes*," they can never feel the pain of failure, so they have developed the behavior habit of simply saying *"I'll try,"* which protects them from the emotional pain they fear.

The words "I'll try" are an escape route for some people

If you look back at the history of people who use the words *"I'll try,"* you will more than likely see a pattern of poor performance. This is because they feel very little accountability or commitment to anyone or anything. As employers, significant others, or parents, we should never allow the people in our lives to use those words because they are disempowering and perpetuate poor performance and behaviors. If we care about these people (and pay attention to ourselves as well), we will listen to the words they use and coach them out of using those words by educating them about the deeper meaning behind them.

Let's go back to my example with the employee who you asked to get you the report by Friday, and they responded with the words *"I'll try."* You should stop when you hear those words and ask them what *"I'll try"* means to them. Have a conversation about those words and educate them about the negative side of that behavior habit they have developed. Let them know that starting right now, they will have four answer options to your questions:

- *Yes*
- *No*
- *Counter offer*
- *May I get back to you about that?*

In other words, they can answer with, *"Yes, I will get you that report on Friday,"* or they can say, *"No, I can't get you that report Friday,"* in which case it would be followed up with a conversation as to why they can't and what could be done. They may also offer a counter offer, such as *"I am incredibly busy through Friday, but I could get it to you Monday, so would that be alright?"* They may also choose to say, *"I need to look at my calendar and compare that to my priorities for the week, so may I get back to you in a couple of hours with an answer?"* These can all be acceptable options depending on how accommodating you want to be, but the words *"I'll try"* should be banished from everyone's vocabulary because they do not serve anyone.

A couple more disempowering words that can be heard in daily conversation are *"**I wish**,"* which might be used like this: *"I wish I could get a new car."* Wishing is thought without action. There is no forward movement with the word *"wish"* because it can sit aimlessly in your brain for lengthy periods of time without requiring any additional thought or plan. To turn something from a wish to reality, you must be committed and have a plan (by setting a S.M.A.R.T. goal and Idea Mapping your goal), so I would suggest replacing *"I wish"* with *"I will"* or *"When."* The words *"I will"* or *"When"* create intrinsic accountability and will help motivate you to action and success.

Using the words *"**I hope**"* is very much like using the words *"I wish"* because it requires no action. You would get the same results if you had desires and just crossed your fingers and hoped they became a reality. One of the only ways for hopes or wishes to become reality is for you to write them down, which would help create personal commitment and accountability. If you at least go through this process, the chance of turning a hope or wish into a reality becomes more realistic.

When you hear someone use the words *"**I can't**,"* which are also very disempowering; think about what their intent might be. Are they expecting to be let off the hook for something by playing the victim? Are they testing you to see how committed you are to whatever it is that they say they can't do? This word is used often, and much of the time it comes from people who feel disempowered, disenfranchised, or have low self-worth (people who give up easily).

As an example, if your teenager comes home from school, slams their books on the table and cries, "*I can't do this homework!*" ask them calmly for clarification. Ask them if they truly cannot do the homework or is their frustration focused on how hard it is. In most cases, they are frustrated or even scared about how difficult the homework is (the anticipation of pain), so they voice it with the words "*I can't.*" It would be really easy for them to continue to say "*I can't*" because it would not require any further action on their part. This is a good example of the reptilian response where they freeze themselves in a place or time. This is where the role of victim begins because they believe there is nothing they can do and that they have no choices available. To unfreeze someone from this place, it may require you to discuss what choices are available to help move the homework forward. The ideas may not be easy or fun, but it moves the project forward to completion. If they attempt to stay frozen in time and repeat the phrase "*I can't,*" then ask them, "*But what if you could? What would that look like?*" This would also be a great opportunity to teach your child the process of Idea Mapping, which we discussed in the last chapter because that is all about creating ideas and possibilities. It breaks down projects into manageable steps and timelines that move them forward to a successful outcome without being overwhelming. Instead of allowing them to stay focused on what they can't do (festering in their misery), get them refocused on what they can do. It is important to be relentless about keeping the door open for possibility.

Another disempowering word we hear a lot is "***someday.***" It is a word commonly used by procrastinators because there is no time frame attached to it, which means there is no personal accountability. If I said, "*Someday I am going to buy investment property in order to help supplement my pension,*" what exactly is my plan? When is someday? Like I have said repeatedly in this book, for many people, someday is like the eighth day of the week that simply never comes. It is a way for us to have a plan in our head, but never having to commit to it. The word "someday" is lazy because it requires no action on your part.

It might also be a way of protecting you from the anticipated emotional pain of failure if you don't end up committing to your plan. Is it possible that "fear" (the anticipation of pain) drives us to inaction, putting off many things simply by using the word "someday"? If you hear yourself, your family or employees use the word "someday," ask them if they would be willing to commit to a specific date. If not, ask them why and you may hear a number of excuses that are designed to keep them from feeling accountable (the fear of failure). Holding people accountable to themselves can be life changing because it may break them of a very disempowering behavior habit that inhibits them from living an extraordinary life and achieving their greatest desires.

Here are some of the possible options for replacing your current bad habit with a positive habit:

- "If.............." *replace it with "When"*
- "I'll try......" *replace it with "Yes"*
- "I wish......." *replace it with "I will" or "When"*
- "I hope......" *replace it with "I will" or "When"*
- "I can't......" *replace it with "I can"*
- "Someday..."*replace it with a specific date because some-day is like the eighth day of the week.*

I mentioned earlier that no thought can live rent free in your head. The "bad habit" words above, if used in your life on a regular basis, will have a dramatic negative impact on you because they have deeper meaning behind them. Some people use these words to keep them from action or to protect themselves from emotional pain and that has everything to do with their self-worth and level of confidence. Either way, these disempowering words freeze you in time and keep you from living the life you deserve. Believe in yourself, believe you have no limits, and believe that anything you want in life is attainable.

Chapter 10

WHERE IS YOUR MOTIVATION
COMING FROM?

Motivation is a huge component to living an extraordinary life and having the things you desire, so where does your motivation come from? Back in Chapter Two, we discussed the emotional motivators that can either motivate us toward change or hold us hostage by creating inaction. The emotional motivators are pain and pleasure; however, emotional pain is the one that controls and dominates us in the decisions we make every day. There are two psychological motivators that control where the emotional motivators come from.

The two psychological motivators:

- *Intrinsic*
- *Extrinsic*

Intrinsic motivation is when power is unleashed within you, and extrinsic motivation is when power is exerted over you. Intrinsic motivation comes from within us and is self imposed, so if you are feeling any of the emotional motivators such as fear, guilt, failure, rejection, humiliation or embarrassment, it means, more than likely, you have created those fears yourself. The question is not about whether they are real or not, because in many cases they are simply stories that our Gremlin is creating to get us to conform and back down from trying new things. The only thing you want to be clear about is that you are creating them and no one else (no outside force). With that said, people, events, or circumstances can certainly influence your thinking and can create some of the stories in your head.

Extrinsic motivation normally comes from other people attempting to influence you in some manner. It might be your supervisor, peers, significant other, children, family, friends or community who are imparting wishes, demands or requests upon you. It might be your supervisor (I intentionally avoid the word "boss" because no one wants to be bossed around, so even though you may have one of these in your life, I am going to avoid the word as a courtesy to the great leaders of the world) who tells you that you must have the annual financial report to them by Friday. Friday may seem very unreasonable to you, but you are feeling the pressure from your supervisor, so you will do everything in your power to make sure they get the report on time. You are now feeling extrinsic pressure to complete the task.

There is another type of extrinsic motivation that occurs in the workplace, which is more passive. If you are a salesperson and your company creates an incentive or bonus plan to motivate you to sell more product, that is extrinsic motivation because the motivation is provided by someone else and not you. In essence, good commissioned salespeople, even though they may be quite self-motivated, are still motivated from an outside source (their commission pay structure). If they do not sell products or services, they are not getting paid. So the company created the motivation for them to perform, which makes it extrinsic. This passive type of extrinsic motivation is not necessarily a bad thing because it is normally put into place since most salespeople will normally perform

Great salespeople come to work passion-driven and self-motivated

at a higher level when incentivized to do so. Great salespeople come to work passion-driven and self-motivated, and if given extrinsic motivation, such as a good commission structure, it simply fuels the fire already within them to perform even better.

Perhaps your significant other is tired of you working late into the evening and working weekends. They are also fed up with you coming home tired and not investing time in them and the relationship, so you are feeling the pressure from them to change your work habits and conform to their desires. You are motivated by their requests, so you alter your work habits, but now you get hit from both sides because your supervisor has noticed the changes and is questioning your commitment to the organization. So now you have extrinsic pressure from both work and home, which is pulling you apart. This is one of the reasons that our lives can feel so stressful today because we are pulled in so many different directions from outside sources. Extrinsic motivation creates pressure because we no longer feel in control of our lives since someone else is exerting the control over us.

Now, let's really pile it on and say your kids are also feeling neglected and want you to attend their soccer games, which are three nights a week and on weekends. You also feel an obligation to attend parent-teacher meetings, dance recitals, and help them with their homework. Your son also asks if you would be the scout master for his Boy Scout Troop because the other fathers are getting involved. Getting stressed yet? This is the feeling of extrinsic motivation, and it can sometimes be overwhelming if coming at you from all sides.

There is another angle to extrinsic motivation, which needs to be addressed. If you are a leader of people, you are probably taught that it is important to keep your employees motivated and happy. I cannot argue with the philosophy because high employee satisfaction is important in the workplace and can be directly attributed to higher profits in many organizations. However, if your employees rely on you to keep them motivated then you are setting yourself and them up for failure. If they rely on you for motivation, which for them is extrinsic motivation because it is coming from you and not them, then what happens if you take a vacation, and you are not around to motivate them? If they become reliant on you to motivate them, and you are not there, are they going to feel unmotivated?

Our role as leaders is to have good systems in place that keep them intrinsically motivated, so we don't have to be the motivators. In other words, we need to proactively work toward creating a fun and productive workplace. That includes having clearly defined service standards and job descriptions, so there is no miscommunication or misunderstanding about what is expected of your employees. It needs to be a workplace where they feel physically and emotionally safe to do their jobs without being micro-managed. The workplace should have a process in place where employees are listened to on a regular basis through roundtable discussions and focus groups, so everyone is heard. It needs to be a place where employees are recognized and rewarded for their performance. We also need to "lead" and not "manage" them, and if we do these things right, they will feel self-motivated to want to do a great job without us having to be actively involved in the act of motivating them every day.

Both intrinsic and extrinsic methods can be powerful motivators, but one will give you personal power, and the other could rob you of it. One is empowering, and the other could be disempowering. One gives you energy, and the other one could drain you of energy. One has you performing with intention and focus while the other could distract and divert your attention. Intrinsic motivation should obviously be the goal not only for us, but for our employees, significant others and children. Anyone who is reliant on someone else for their feelings, emotions or motivation could become handicapped and would be a great candidate to become a victim, frozen in time when their "motivator" is not around. Make sure that the choices you make in your life are coming primarily from you and not those around you. If someone else is trying to motivate you to change by exerting their control over you, it will eventually lead to resentment, and that will eventually turn into retaliation. You might be able to handle this type of control over you for a while, and you might even justify why it is acceptable to you, but that cannot last forever. Yes, some people might influence your decisions from time to time, which is not always a bad thing. However, make sure your motivation comes primarily from within in order to stay in possession of your personal power, which is what is required to have an extraordinary career and life, and achieve your greatest desires.

Chapter 11

LIFE IS ALL ABOUT CHOICES

There is nothing more powerful than personal responsibility and accountability. If you don't like your circumstances, choose to <u>change them</u>. Every waking moment is about choices and the rewards or consequences attached to them. Every single day, whether in our personal or business life, we are put into circumstances that require us to make decisions and make choices. Some of them are easy, and some of them require tremendous thought, and that is because every choice we make comes with two variables:

1. *Rewards (pleasure)*

2. *Consequences (pain)*

Even the simplest decisions, such as whether or not you are going to put the trash out tonight, come with weighing the rewards and consequences of your choices. If you choose not to put the garbage out to the curb tonight, the garbage collector will not be able to collect it in the morning, and since it is full, you will not have room in the can for the next week's garbage. Your garbage sitting for another week, getting smelly and overflowing would be the consequence of choosing to not take it out tonight. If you choose to take the garbage to the curb tonight, then there will be no inconvenience to you over the next week, and life is sweet (not to mention sweet smelling).

As another example: in the summer when the lawn is growing fast and furiously and you are tired of mowing it twice a week, you might try to talk yourself into mowing the lawn only once a week. So now you begin to weigh your options. Mowing it twice a week is a big time commitment and takes about two hours every time you mow it. You have to dump the lawn clippings from the bag about ten times while you are mowing the lawn each time, but other than that, the job is pretty effortless. If you choose to only mow the lawn once a week, instead of twice, what are the rewards? The only reward is that you think you will have an extra two hours a week to do something else that you would enjoy doing more. The consequences for mowing it only once a week is that the lawn will be twice as long and twice as hard to mow. Because the grass is twice as long, it will require you to dump the lawn clippings 20 times during each mow, which will slow you down horribly. Since the grass is so long, the mower would be harder to push and also tend to jam the blades and bag, which you have to stop and clean out every couple minutes. After thinking it through, it will not save you any time, and the consequences are far greater than the rewards, so you may continue to mow the lawn twice a week.

If you think about how many large and small choices we make each day, it must be hundreds, if not a thousand. The big ones might require days, weeks or even months, so there is no time frame controlling choices. Some of them are made at a subconscious level and require very little analysis because they are decided for us based on our previous experiences. However, they still require a quick analysis as to the rewards and consequences of our actions. If you look back at some of the quick choices you have made, which you gave very little thought to, you might remember that you wish you would have given more consideration to the rewards and consequences. If you go back to Chapter Four, you might remember the section about the

Reptilian Brain and how we might be prone to making quick and automated responses, without enough consideration to the rewards and consequences of our decisions. That is why it is important to give your entire brain time to process the rewards and consequences of the choices you make and if you do that, you will make the best choices for you.

Choice is all about personal power, which is the ultimate expression of free will. Even though people, events or circumstances can influence your choices, no one can make choices for you unless you allow them to. One way you might lose your right to choice is if you make a bad choice; break the law, and the consequence of your action results in incarceration. Even though you still have many choices to make each day, they may be limited because you gave up your rights to a few of them by your earlier poor choice. If you end up in this circumstance, then you certainly need to re-evaluate your decision making process because even though you may have given lots of consideration to the rewards of your illegal actions, you obviously did not give equal consideration to the consequences of your actions.

Some of you will choose to apply what you have learned in this book and will be rewarded with an extraordinary life, and you will more than likely also achieve your greatest desires. Some of you will make the decision that these steps are just too much work, or decide you are not willing to change and will continue the same path you are on. The definition of insanity is continuing to do things the way you have always done them and expecting better results tomorrow. The problem may be that you cannot envision the rewards for changing your life because your Gremlin is not allowing you to see yourself in a place of success, power, wealth or happiness. How can you imagine being in a fabulous relationship, completely immersed in the perfect love, if you have never seen or been involved in such a relationship before? Maybe the thought of owning a gorgeous home or even a yacht is so far out of the realm of possibility for you that you are willing to give up your personal power and not follow through with the steps in this book. Your lack of vision may fall under the category of, "You don't know what you don't know."

Let me explain the last sentence above so that you can understand the idea behind it because I know it sounds confusing. There are things that "We know that we know." In other words, I know that I know how to drive a car, use a computer, do a keynote speech, water ski and play golf. I know how to do those things, and I know it. Then there are things "We know that we don't know." In other words, I know that I do not know how to operate a nuclear plant. I also know that I don't know how to fly a jet plane because I have never been trained. I also know that I don't know how to do brain surgery, and I guarantee you would not want me to "give it a shot." These are things that I am very clear about, in terms of knowing that I know I do not know how to do them. There are also things that "We don't know what we don't know." If you have never had a business partner, you would never know to have a "Buy-Sell Agreement" because you have never been in the circumstance before. If you had never been a professional speaker before, you would never know that it is important to arrive at least an hour before each speech to do a sound and audio check, plus check the lighting. If you had never owned a yacht before, you would never know to check the Sea Strainers often to keep your engine coolant working properly. How can you possibly know these things if you have never experienced them before?

Many people struggle with imagining themselves as successful, powerful, wealthy or even madly in love because they have never experienced it before. They find safe refuge in maintaining their current life, no matter how dismal or unfulfilling it may be because they cannot see beyond the walls that surround them. These walls are like a prison that the Gremlin has created because these walls help the Gremlin control you and keep you exactly where you are (frozen in time). If you choose to not follow the steps in this book, then that is a happy day for the Gremlin because it will require no action and no change. If at the end of this book, you put it on your bookshelf along with the rest of your collection of self-help books to never be seen again, please consider that it may be the Gremlin who is making that choice for you. If you do not choose to learn to manage the Gremlin, it will continue to manage you.

If you love your life as it is today and your desires are completely fulfilled, then give your Gremlin a hug and let it continue to manage your life. However, if you want more from life, now is the time to take control and make better choices. That is why I have always loved the quote by William Johnson, "*If it is to be, it is up to me!*"

Many people struggle with imagining themselves as successful, powerful, wealthy or even madly in love because they have never experienced it before.

As you are confronted with choices in your life, pay attention to who is making them for you because it may not just be the Gremlin. It may be your supervisor, your peers, your significant other, your children, your family, your friends, your community or any combination thereof (by their demands or influence). Why would you let someone else write the script for your life? Why would you give any other person or thing (Gremlin) that much control over the direction of your life? This is the day and time to step up to the plate and take responsibility for yourself and the choices you make. There may be times when you don't trust yourself, but no one knows you better than you. If you leave your future in anyone else's hands, you have stepped into the role of a victim because you have given up your personal power, and now you are along for "their" ride, not your own.

Back in about 1983, when I was Operations Manager for a chain of retail clothing stores in the Seattle, Washington area, I had a great General Manager over me who was incredibly smart and kind-hearted. He was a great family man, soft spoken and treated everyone with ultimate respect. One day, he asked me why something had not been done that he had requested of me. I was telling him about all the other things I had to do that diverted me away from his request. I can remember going through the long list and saying, "*I have to do this, and I have to do that*," and after listening to me for a few minutes, he calmly stopped me mid-sentence.

He said to me, "*Do you know that there is nothing you have to do but die?*" For a moment I thought that this was becoming a very morbid conversation, but I continued to listen with interest. He told me that life is simply a series of choices, and the ones we make will either have rewards or consequences. He asked me if there was anything that I actually had to do, which I had no choice over. I told him that I have to pay taxes and he told me that was not true. He asked me what would happen if I chose to not pay my taxes, and I told him I would probably end up going to jail. So he said; "So, *you actually do have a choice.*" One is to not pay taxes, and the consequence would be for me to go to jail, and the other choice is to continue to pay them and be rewarded with freedom. I agreed with that scenario, but I just knew there were things that I had no choice over so I continued to try to prove him wrong.

I told him that I had to eat, and he told me that eating was a choice. He asked me what would happen if I stopped eating, and I told him I would probably die (point made). I tried to get clever and trick him by telling him that I had to breathe, and he said breathing was a choice. If you choose to not breathe, simply put your head under water and you will more than likely stop. I told him that kids are required by law to go to school every day, so they certainly don't have a choice in that. He told me that they certainly do have a choice and if they choose to not go to school, what would happen? I told him they would probably not get educated, not get a diploma, which may lead to them not getting a job, which means they can't buy food and support themselves, which means they may end up dead. Dang! He got me again!

I have been thinking about that conversation since that day, and I have not been able to think of anything that we have to do but die. Everything truly is a choice with rewards or consequences as the result of our decision. I tell this same story in one of my seminars and ask the attendees if they can think of anything that they have to do, and no one has been able to come up with anything either. The closest anyone came is when I was in North Carolina doing a seminar for branch managers of a bank and a woman in the front row said, *"Having a bowel movement!"* The place broke into laughter for about ten minutes. My response was, *"If you choose to not have a bowel movement, you may wish you were dead."*

The misperception that you have no choice can lead people into feeling trapped and can sometimes lead to depression. A trapped perspective leads to feelings of helplessness, anxiety or apathy and can freeze people in time and normally not in a good place. In order to help free yourself from a trapped perspective, you might try using some of the Gremlin's own controlling words ("But what if…") and turn them around for your benefit by reframing them into a positive point of view. If you think you have no options available to you in a circumstance, trying asking yourself the question, *"But what if I could and what would that look like?"*

In other words, let's just say you are self-employed and you have always wanted to take a two-week vacation. However, you have not had any vacation for three years because you don't have anyone who can answer the phones and handle things while you are gone for two weeks. Instead of staying frozen in time with the idea that there is nothing you can do, ask yourself the questions, *"But what if I could take a two-week vacation? What would that look like?"* Instead of being rigid in your thinking, open up your mind to alternate possibilities, even if they are not exactly what you had envisioned.

If the biggest issue is that you don't have anyone to answer your phones while you are gone and you cannot afford an employee, "what if" you hired an answering service for the time you are gone? They can let your customers know you are on vacation, take a message and let them know you will call them as soon as you return. Maybe two consecutive weeks of vacation is too long to be away because your customers cannot go that long without your services, but "what if" you took two one-week vacations instead? Let's just say that you are a plumber or tow truck operator and are known for being on call 7-days-a-week and 24-hours-a-day, so getting any time off is nearly impossible. "What if" you contacted a friendly competitor to your business and created a partnership to assist each other during your vacations and days off? Instead of focusing on what can't be done, focus on what could be done and open up some new possibilities for yourself.

Choice = Possibility = Opportunity = Success

Choice frees you from a trapped perspective and allows you to participate in your own destiny by increasing your range of options. Sometimes being in the trenches and looking up at the decisions you have to make can be daunting (analysis causes paralysis). So imagine yourself up in a helicopter looking down at the situation and taking a different view of it. Try to look at the big picture, and do not get hung up on why you can't do something. Creating choices will open up possibilities and create opportunity, which will ultimately lead to an extraordinary career and life, and achieving your greatest desires.

Chapter 12

ATTITUDE IS A CHOICE

Have you ever written a letter or e-mail and proofread it multiple times believing it was perfect? Then you asked someone else to proof it for you, and they found multiple mistakes. How is it possible that you read it over and over again, and you could not see your mistakes? The question becomes, were you reading what you actually wrote or what you thought you wrote (what you wanted to see)? Is it possible that we live our lives this same way and that we see life the way we want to see it and not the way it actually is?

I wake up every day happy and feeling tremendous gratitude for all the gifts in my life, from finding true love, good health, great family and friends, a job that I love, living in beautiful Washington State and many other things that I embrace. Is that the way the world actually is or is that the way I choose to see it? Of course it is the way I see it because many people come to Washington State, as an example, and see the gray clouds and rain and cannot imagine living here. I see a gray and rainy winter day as a great opportunity to relax in front of the fireplace and watch a great movie with a bowl of popcorn and hot buttered rum. I spend much of my day looking for the great things in my life and feeling fortunate for what I have, and I spend very little time, if any, focused on what I don't have.

Some people wake up in the morning and say "*I have to go to work;*" while I get up in the morning and say "*I get to go to work.*" You can try to rationalize your language by saying that my job as a professional speaker is fun and your job is not fun. However, I chose my job and very methodically created my profession and my life through all the steps I talk about in this book. I never played the victim role by blaming my life or lack of job fulfillment on anyone else; I created my own destiny. I have had many jobs in my life that I did not think were fun, such as forest fire fighter, plywood mill worker, green chain operator in a hardwood mill, gas station attendant and others. However, each job taught me one more life lesson about what I did and did not want to do for a living. They helped me focus my choices more in order to make better long-term decisions for my future. I was also willing to take many emotional risks throughout the years to end up with an extraordinary life, so it did not come without sacrifice. I wake up every day with a great attitude because I choose to and because I made many great choices along the way that have led me to where I am today.

There are also people who wake up every day believing the world is full of prejudice, anger, bigotry, hatred and many other societal ills. I am not trying to say that these things do not exist in our world, because they certainly do – but does that then become how we see the world? Even if the world changes and we eradicate these things from society, will our perception of the world ever allow us to see the changes? Will we continue to see the world through our own lenses? Will you continue to walk around with a chip on your shoulder and play the victim even if the world changes? The biggest question is: how does that serve you?

Your attitude is the lens by which you see the world around you (your mental focus). You can choose to see the world through a lens that allows you to see a land of opportunity and freedom. The world can be a place of happiness where dreams can come true, and the only limits are the ones you place on yourself. Or, you can choose a different lens, one that sees the world as a place where politicians are corrupt, and the news is full of violence where people have a low regard for human life. You can choose to see a place that binds you by its laws and restricts you from doing what you want to do. These lenses have you focused on the things that are wrong with the world, leaving you

> *No one has the power to change your attitude unless you "choose" to give them that power*

skeptical, disheartened and doubtful that things will get any better. The lens you choose each day shapes your attitude, and both your lens and attitude are a choice. No one has the power to change your attitude unless you "choose" to give them that power (you would be giving up your personal power). When you are waking up in the morning and trying to decide what kind of attitude you want for the day, consider the results that are triggered when you focus on either a positive or negative attitude:

- **Positive attitudes:**
  - *Happy*
  - *Give energy*
  - *Inspire others*
  - *See opportunity*
  - *Foster creativity*
  - *Build enthusiasm*
  - *Attract people to you*
  - *Create serendipitous good fortune*

If you choose to wake up and have a positive attitude, you will not only be happy and have more energy yourself, but you will be infectious and spread your positive energy to others. People love to associate with those who give them energy and make them feel good about themselves. Your positive attitude inspires other people, so they want to be like you – you have the ability to change other's attitudes based on your own. You also see the world through a powerful lens, which is the one that sees opportunity around each corner. You see potential in the world that people with negative attitudes do not see – you create opportunity for yourself.

A positive attitude also fosters more creativity in our personal and professional lives. Creativity frees us from the confines of normal thinking and allows us to make better choices. It keeps our mind healthy and our cardiovascular system energized, which keeps our creative juices flowing. Our enthusiasm is a result of our energy and the way people respond to it. People are attracted to positive and energetic people, so your choice for a positive attitude has tremendous radial impact. All the things listed above under "positive attitudes" create serendipitous good fortune, not just for you, but for the people around you.

Another benefit to having a positive attitude is your health. After having spent plenty of time at the Seattle Cancer Care Alliance over the last few years with Melanie and her journey with pancreatic cancer, I truly believe her attitude has been one of the keys to her survival. As mentioned earlier in the book, only 4 percent of the people who get diagnosed with pancreatic cancer survive beyond five years and Melanie is one of them. We decided very early on that if 4 percent survive beyond five years, then someone has to be one of the lucky 4 percent, so we decided that she would be one of them (we chose a positive attitude in the face of adversity). Her attitude from day one has always been incredibly positive. Anytime she would start to waiver and the Gremlin would start to create negative stories in her head, I would remind her that the majority of the things we worry about never come true, so don't spend time on negative thoughts (it is the Gremlin telling its fables again). Our fabulous oncologist at the Seattle Cancer Care Alliance, Dr. Edward Lin, concurred that a positive attitude indeed can have an effect on cancer survival. So beside all the other fabulous benefits to having a positive attitude, being healthy and living longer are great benefits to consider.

- ***Negative attitudes:***
  - *Unhappy*
  - *Drain energy*
  - *Impact others*
  - *Miss opportunity*
  - *Stifle creativity*
  - *Crush enthusiasm*
  - *Repel people away from you*
  - *Create an environment of poor luck*

If you choose to wake up and have a negative attitude and be unhappy, the drain of energy begins not only just for yourself, but for everyone you come into contact with. Energy is infectious, so energy drain spreads rapidly and impacts not only everyone's attitude but productivity as well, and in a business environment, it can impact profitability too. People, who see the world through a negative lens, see the wrong with the world and miss the right with the world. They miss opportunity because they are tuned out to the potential that exists around them. Opportunity is invisible to people with negative attitudes, so life becomes stagnant.

Negative attitudes, because of their energy draining capabilities, stifle creativity and can create emotional paralysis. This is a state where your options feel limited and as we have learned with "choice," the lack of choice can lead to the feelings of victimization. Due to your lack of energy, you will crush your own enthusiasm and that of those around you, which will repel people from you. No one wants to hang around Energy Vampires, so you will find yourself with few friends and even fewer supporters. The end result of all of this is an environment of perceived poor luck, even though there is no luck involved at all because it is the result of the poor choice of choosing a negative attitude.

If you choose to wake up and have a negative attitude, you need to consider the radial impact of your choice. If you do not go to work and plan on sitting home all day and avoiding people, then the damage is pretty minimal because you are the only one who is going to suffer from your poor choice. However, if you have to go to work, then give serious consideration to your attitude choice because it impacts other people. To not give consideration to your attitude at this point makes you very self-centered because you are only focused on you and not others. You are so wrapped up in your own misery that you cannot see the damage that your attitude is having on others.

Let me ask you a question: If you worked in an office with ten co-workers and one of them comes to work with a negative attitude, is it possible you would feel the impact? Of course you would, and more than likely, so will everyone else. If you wake up in the morning mad because you have to go to work, it is like drinking poison and hoping someone else will die. It does not serve you. The old saying *"one rotten apple can spoil the whole batch"* is very true in this case. Negative attitudes become distractions that interfere with focus and productivity. Positive attitudes in the workplace produce fewer mistakes, higher quality work, better productivity and a more fun work environment, which is very important to everyone.

Since attitude is a choice, let's look at some of the choices you make and see if you have an attitude that serves you and the world well. Answer the following questions with complete honesty:

1. *Do you graciously allow cars to merge in front of you in traffic?*

2. *Do you stop to allow people to safely cross a street, even without a crosswalk?*

3. *Do you occasionally open doors for complete strangers?*

4. *Do you always sincerely thank employees when they serve you?*

5. In a grocery store parking lot, would you help someone struggling with bags?

6. If someone spilled a box full of books on the ground, would you offer to help?

7. If a stranger was short 50 cents in a checkout line, would you give it to them?

8. If you were riding a packed subway, would you offer your seat to a senior?

9. If a bank teller gave you $20 too much, would you let them know?

10. Are you in a good mood at least 90 percent of the time?

So what did you learn about you? Are you selfless or selfish? In the case of question #1 above, what is the payoff to you for not letting someone merge in front of you in traffic? In other words, what is the benefit to you for trying to keep someone from merging into traffic, assuming they have put their blinker on and done everything right? If a 21-year-old man was standing on a corner wanting to cross the street, and there wasn't a cross-walk, stop sign or traffic light, would you still stop and allow him to safely cross? If not, once again, what is the payoff to you for not allowing him to cross? What if that person was you? How would you feel if no one would let you cross the street? What if it was a young woman with a baby stroller? Would it make any difference?

We have all had circumstances where we are pulling on to a freeway when we see a gap in traffic large enough to merge between the cars. We place our blinker on, check our side mirror one more time before changing lanes, and watch a car speed up to close the gap to keep us from merging. Why on earth would they do that? And how does that serve them? Do they get a rush of adrenaline, feeling of control, power, dominance or what? I will tell you that I would never want to be married to someone like that because I will guarantee that is how they are in other areas of their life as well. If that has ever happened to you, why on earth would you ever do that to anyone else knowing how you felt about that inconsiderate person?

I will give you my perspective on those same questions. I will go out of my way to do whatever I can to allow people to merge, cross streets, open a door or help a stranger, and the payoff for me is that it makes me feel good. The act of serving others provides me with a gift that cannot be bought, and that is the gift of self-respect. I am always looking for ways to exceed people's expectations, which is also the title of my first book *(The Ultimate Guide to Exceeding Customer Expectations)*. I do it because it not only makes other people feel good, but it makes me feel good as well, so what a huge pay off for everyone. These actions are the difference between selfless and selfish, and all I can ask is that you give consideration to the answers on the attitude assessment above. If needed, re-think how you might respond in the future and how it might serve you better. Also ask yourself on each of those questions: where else in your life are those choices present? The last question to ask yourself is: do you think that selfless or selfish actions will help you live an extraordinary life and achieve your greatest desires?

As much as I am a firm believer that attitude is a choice, I also realize that there are things that can influence your attitude, or your choice of an attitude. So let's take a look at some of the things that can influence your attitude:

- *People*
- *Events*
- *Circumstances*

People can influence your attitude, and my encouragement to you is to always take the high road and do not get pulled over to the dark side by someone else's behavior or attitude. Do not let anyone take you over emotionally; remove yourself from those situations if needed. No one has the power to take you over emotionally unless you grant them that power, and you should never allow it. You are the only person who has control over your emotions and attitude, which are both a choice, even though they are not always easy choices.

If you end up in a state of conflict, whether it is an argument with a significant other, family member, child, friend, co-worker or supervisor, you should do everything in your power to resolve it quickly. Time does not always heal all wounds, and conflict, if not resolved quickly, can fester like a bad wound and become an even larger problem. Most conflict comes as a result of poor communication, which can be a lack of communication, miscommunication or a poorly communicated message. Poor communication or the lack of understanding about communication can lead to upsets, so let's discuss the different types of upsets and how they occur:

Five primary causes for upsets:

1. *Unfulfilled expectations that __you__ create*

2. *Unfulfilled expectations that __they__ create*

3. *Undelivered communication*

4. *Abandoned intentions*

5. *Issues from the past*

Whenever you feel "**upset**," analyze where the upset is coming from before you verbalize your feelings. Most upsets come from one of the five primary causes below:

Unfulfilled Expectations That You Create:

Example: It is Valentine's Day, and you created a vision of your boyfriend getting down on one knee and proposing to you at your favorite restaurant in romantic candlelight. You ended up with a gift card to a spa and dinner at a different restaurant.

- *Your significant other still created a very nice event, but it was not the event **YOU** had created in your mind. Is it fair to punish people for stories that **YOU** create?*

Unfulfilled Expectations That They Create:

Example: If someone said they wanted to meet you at 1 p.m. and they showed up at 1:30; that might create an upset for you. If someone promised you roses and handed you tulips, that might create an upset for you.

- *Before you react to either, simply ask yourself if **THEY** created the expectation, or did **YOU** create the expectation?*

Undelivered Communication:

Example: There was a new sales promotion being launched today by the marketing department, but they failed to tell you that there were promotional materials and special product in the back room that needed to be put out before the store opened.

- *The lack of communication can cause many upsets, but the goal should be to focus on what system failed that caused the upset in the first place.*

Abandoned Intentions:

Example: You always give your employees a bonus at the end of the year, but you just lost your biggest customer, and business is struggling to the point where you can't pay them a bonus this year. Now they are upset.

- *Even though you have the best intentions, if they get abandoned without proper communication, it can still cause upsets.*

Issues From The Past:

Example: You had just gone through a divorce because your spouse had a drinking problem that ruined your marriage. You have a new relationship that is going great until they order a cocktail at dinner and now you get mad at them.

- *Many upsets come from our past experiences. Were you upset about **THAT** person having a cocktail or was it about your past marriage and your ex-spouse's drinking problem?*

Take responsibility quickly for what you can and apologize if needed, or open up the lines of communication to find out where the problem lies, so it can be resolved quickly. Seek solutions and not blame in order to resolve conflict peacefully.

Avoid internalizing other people's problems because it does not serve either one of you. You can be a great partner, parent, friend, peer or employer by being a good listener, but avoid letting others' problems or drama impact your attitude, or worse yet, your health. This is especially hard to do if you are a parent because you care so deeply for what concerns your children. However, the effects of your attitude can be negative for both of you. Ultimately, you are still accountable for your own attitude, and your positive attitude can also help others recover from their issues faster.

If you have Energy Vampires in your life, it is your responsibility to insulate yourself from their negative power. It is harder to do at work because you may not have control over who you work with. In your personal life, you have far more control over who might impact your attitude. The most difficult circumstance you might face is if this person is a family member and then distancing yourself becomes much more challenging. The goal is to insulate or distance yourself as best you can from their influence, so they do not negatively impact your attitude.

Events can influence your attitude, so try to focus on positive results or outcomes. What is the best case scenario for the event that has occurred? And how much control do I have over the outcome? One of the best philosophies that my father imparted to me over the years was "*Don't cry over spilled milk.*" As an example, when I was 16 years old, I got into a bad car accident, and my new car was wrecked (it was the other driver's fault…no, really). After the accident, my father's only concern was my safety because the car could be replaced. Once he confirmed that I was not hurt, he let me know that there was no sense in worrying about the wrecked car because it was too late to change the results. He said we can't undo what has been done;

instead, we can try to learn from what happened and move on with life. This falls into line with focusing on the things you have control over and not on the things that you don't. There are so many things in life and at work that we have no control over. They are sometimes decisions that are made for us, so what is the pay off for letting them negatively impact our attitude and ruin our day? Sometimes you simply have to let it go.

Circumstances can influence your attitude, although sometimes you might want to accept the concept that *"Stuff happens, deal with it."* Since circumstances are in most cases uncontrollable, accept what has happened and focus on how you plan on dealing with it and what emotion you will choose to attach to it. At best, you might be able to consider what lesson is in it for you. As hard as it might be at times, the key is to focus on the door opening ahead of you and not on the one closing behind you. Because negative circumstances are a reality of life, sometimes the key is how fast you can recover from them.

You can't control everything that can impact your attitude, but you can control your attitude. A positive attitude should not be an act; it is a genuine way of viewing your life and the things that can impact your attitude. I have said it many times: I choose a positive attitude every single day, but it is not an act and not something I have to work hard at. Over time, I have created a positive attitude habit, so I do not have to manage the process. It is the way I choose to wake up each day and how I choose to live my life. I have weighed the rewards versus consequences of having both a positive and a negative attitude. I cannot see any reason on earth why I would not choose to wake up and greet each day with anything less than a genuinely positive attitude.

Summary of things that can influence your attitude:

- *People*
  - *Take the high road*
  - *Resolve conflict quickly*

- ○ *Don't internalize other people's problems*
- ○ *Insulate or distance yourself from negative people*
- *Events*
    - ○ *Focus on positive results*
    - ○ *Don't cry over spilled milk*
    - ○ *Focus on the things you have control over, not the things you don't*
- *Circumstances*
    - ○ *Stuff happens, deal with it*
    - ○ *Consider what the lesson is*
    - ○ *Focus on the door ahead of you opening instead of the one behind you closing*

To summarize the "Attitude is a Choice" chapter, we have already talked about how confidence is one of the differences between the rich and the poor. I also believe it is the primary catalyst for living an extraordinary life and achieving your greatest desires. I would like to pose a question: isn't confidence also an attitude? It is certainly the main reason that tall people will make more money over their lifetime (because they naturally appear to have more confidence due to their height). If you believe confidence is an attitude and attitude is a choice, then why on earth wouldn't you want to choose to be confident if the rewards are so great? The dictionary definition of confidence is *"belief in your own abilities; a belief or self assurance in your ability to succeed."* Once you develop a behavior habit of truly believing in yourself (self confidence), you are one step closer to having an extraordinary career and life, and achieving your greatest desires!

Chapter 13

SYMPTOMS VS. PROBLEMS

You probably noticed back in Chapter 4 (Understanding Fear) a lot of conversation around the words "symptom" and "problem." We are very poor at diagnosing ourselves because we perceive most of our symptoms as problems. As an example, if you are driving down the freeway, and all of a sudden your engine stops leaving you stuck along the side of the road, is that a symptom or a problem? Ninety-five percent of the attendees in my seminar audiences, when asked that question, will answer that it is a problem. However, it is actually a symptom because the problem is that your engine is no longer working. The specific problem could be that you ran out of gas, forgot to put oil or water into the engine, or there could be a number of other reasons why the engine stopped. So even though it feels like a problem, and your brain is saying it is a problem, it is actually a symptom, and you need to locate the specific problem.

As another example, let's say you are the owner of five retail stores, and you have managers overseeing each of the locations. Business has been good, and the entire operation seems to be stable. All of a sudden you have employees at one of your locations starting to give notice that they are quitting. Is that a problem or a symptom?

This one is a little easier than the last, and you are right – it is a symptom, and you need to identify the problem. You have probably figured out that if employees are quitting in one store, it normally means you have a leadership problem in that location. More than likely you have a manager who is "managing" the employees or who has done something that the employees do not like. In this case, I would immediately contact the employees and do interviews to find out what the problem actually is.

A few months ago, I woke up in the morning and was feeling stressed, which is not normal for me. My brain quickly diagnosed that it was a symptom (most people would view it as a problem, because it feels bad), so I began to self-analyze why I was feeling poorly. Turns out I had a busy week coming up and had self-doubt about whether I was completely prepared or not. The uncertainty about whether I had all my airline and hotel reservations confirmed, seminar handouts prepared and PowerPoint presentations customized, left me with anxiety (which felt stressful). Once I had self-diagnosed that it was the lack of clarity or the feelings of uncertainty, I went to my office, opened my calendar and travel folder and went through each day to see if I had everything in order. It took me about ten minutes, but once I determined that I had indeed done everything that I was supposed to do, my stress completely disappeared, and life was back to normal.

The challenge with "problems" is that we feel the "symptoms" and our brain labels them as problems. This can divert our attention and misdirect us, making it hard to get to the root of the problem. Here are just a few symptoms that commonly get misdiagnosed:

- *Sad*
- *Angry*
- *Hostile*
- *Jealous*
- *Nervous*
- *Irritable*
- *Depressed*
- *Tense*
- *Guilty*
- *Afraid*
- *Anxious*
- *Stressed*
- *Annoyed*
- *Embarrassed*

When you are experiencing any of the above symptoms, it certainly feels like a problem, so it is in your best interest to drill down and find out what the problem actually is in order to deal with the problem and not the symptom. Even though we have been talking about emotional symptoms, this philosophy certainly also relates to physical symptoms and problems as well.

A good example might be if you felt a tingling or pain in your arm. Because it is painful, it feels like a problem, and you want it to go away. You try to find a cure for what you think is the problem, so you apply ice, which does not work. Then you take pain medication, which works for a while until it wears off, and the pain comes back

The challenge with "problems" is that we feel the "symptoms"

again. You try massaging the arm to no avail and even try a heating pad thinking that may solve the problem. You have given it your best effort and nothing seems to be solving the problem. That is because the arm is not the problem – it is a symptom. The problem is that your spine is out of alignment and a disc is pinching a nerve that goes to your arm, which is causing the pain. The symptom (pain) is 18 inches away from the problem (pinched nerve). This is the challenge with self diagnosis. It just doesn't always make sense to us because sometimes we don't see the full range of possibilities.

If you have an increased heart rate, sweaty palms, upset stomach, shaking, flushed face, swelling or any other physical symptom, there is often a problem that is causing these symptoms. If you focus on the symptom and try to fix just the symptom, you will fall short until you determine what the problem actually is. As an example, taking pain medication can make you feel better because it masks the pain, but it may not resolve the problem. This wasted time through misdirection can actually escalate the symptom and make the problem worse.

The point of this chapter is to create awareness about your feelings and emotions by becoming clear as to their source. Your brain will instinctively try to label everything a "problem" because that is what it feels like. It will get you so wrapped up in the emotion that you are dealing with that you will not be able to locate and address the actual problem. It truly wastes your time by redirecting your attention and draining you of energy. When you wake up in the morning, do a quick body scan and see if you have any of the symptoms listed above, and if you do, locate the source and deal with it immediately (find solutions and not excuses) so you can get back on the path to having an extraordinary career and life, and achieving your greatest desires.

Chapter 14

DOES YOUR PAST INFLUENCE
YOUR FUTURE?

Absolutely! As we discussed in Chapter 6, the Gremlin more than likely evolved because of an emotional wound from your early childhood days. The Gremlin will continue to remind us of our emotional wounds or our imperfections that we collect in our journey through life. People, circumstances and events can have dramatic influences on our future; however, they are not always negative.

I will never forget when I was about 21 years old and the mother of a girl I was dating looked me in the eyes at one point during dinner and told me that she knew I was going to have a great future. I don't remember the exact words, but I remember that look of sincerity in her eyes when she told me that I was destined for greatness. I felt my chest swell with pride, but I also felt tears wanting to push their way to the surface because it felt so good to have someone validate what I believed in myself. As much as the Gremlin has tried to convince me that I am not good enough throughout my life, those words from a non-family member always stuck with me. The interesting thing is that my family was very supportive and always offered praise, but it was the unsolicited words of someone outside the family that seemed to resonate the most. This is a good example of how important it is to let people hear the good things about themselves because it may have a positive long-lasting impact.

For me, offering sincere praise to others is part of living an extraordinary life, and I look for every opportunity to do so. Remember, one of our primal fears is not being good enough, so when you have a complete stranger tell you that you are special or that you have a gift, it has tremendous meaning. I was recently in Lake Chelan, Washington, doing a seminar for the Chamber of Commerce, and I went to a well-known restaurant in town to have dinner before the event. I walked in and was greeted by the approximately 22-year-old hostess who had an infectious smile and an amazing personality. She sat me at a table, where I watched her greet other customers, and when she was not doing that, she would stay busy cleaning tables and doing other busy work. From her perspective, she was probably just doing her job, but from my perspective, she was the perfect employee for that particular job (great hiring by someone).

Later that evening, I came back to the restaurant to sit outside the bar and have a glass of wine and relax before going to sleep. This young lady was still working just as hard as she had been four hours earlier. Every customer with whom this young lady interacted, left with a huge smile on their face and a bounce in their step because of this employee's tremendous personality and charm. As the restaurant slowed down and was getting ready to close, she stopped to ask me if I needed anything else, so I asked her if she had a couple of extra minutes, to which she replied, "*Yes.*"

I told her that she had a tremendous gift, and she should not take it lightly. She was blessed with an innate gift to be able to tap into other people's emotions. I told her that with the combination of her fabulous smile, great personality and excellent work ethic, there was nothing in life that she was not going to be able to achieve. I told her that only a small percentage of people on this earth have her gift and that she was going to have an amazing future. I told her no one comes into your life by accident, and I wanted her to remember this moment because I want her to reflect back on it whenever she starts to have self-doubt.

She listened to me in silence and then her eyes began to well up with tears. She thanked me and told me she had gone to college for a couple of years, but she was confused, in self-doubt and could not decide what to get a degree in. She had moved back home with her parents and was working at the restaurant until she figured out what to do next. Based on our conversation, she said she now wanted to go back to college, get a business degree and pursue a career.

As each of us has a Gremlin that tries to keep us from greatness, I hope we are all lucky enough to also have a supportive voice that we can reflect back on to remind us that we are special. I truly hope that each of you looks for opportunities to make a significant positive impact on the people around you, not only family and friends, but also people you might meet randomly in life. This can only be achieved if it is a completely selfless act from which you seek nothing in return. Your reward should simply be that you made a difference in someone's life. Hopefully, the person whose life you touched will pay it forward by their kind words and change someone else's life in the future as well.

Unfortunately, negative people, events and circumstances are much easier to remember because they normally leave the deepest emotional scars. As humans, we are prone to negative thought more than positive thought, so the negative influences unfortunately play a larger role in our lives. A good example of that is when I ask seminar attendees to rate my presentations on a scale of 1 to 10 at the end of each event in a paper survey. Most of the scores are 9 or 10 and the average rating for most of my events is about 9.7 (taking the total of all scores and dividing them by the number of attendees). However, every so often, someone will score me under 5 and leave no explanation as to why (which leaves a lot of unanswered questions). Out of the 500 responses from that event, I get only one low score, but guess which score I toil over on my commute home? I beat myself up the whole way home trying to think about what I could have done differently and why that person scored me so low. I completely forgot about the other 499 fabulous scores.

Because we tend to focus on the bad things, my request to all of you is to avoid leaving victims in your wake. This means that you should watch the words you use with others and make sure they do not leave emotional wounds. We need to be cautious to avoid participating in events that might have a negative impact on someone's self-worth. We should also avoid circumstances that might leave emotional tolls on people, because once the words leave our lips, they are very hard to take back, and the damage is done. This is especially true of children because they are so impressionable. Inconsiderate or misdirected words can leave scars that can last forever, so always speak in a thoughtful manner.

When I talk about avoiding circumstances that can leave emotional wounds, it is not just about being cautious of the words we use but cautious with your actions as well. As an example, the memories of a significant other cheating on you will be with you for a long time, and those thoughts can make you cautious and in turn, alter your future behavior. Let's say you loved and trusted someone completely for the last 15 years and had no reason to ever believe they would violate that trust. Then you find out the person has been having an affair behind your back for a year and lied repeatedly to your face about places they had been and what they had been doing. If a person, who says they have loved you for 15 years and swore they would never do anything to hurt you violates your trust, then how can you trust anyone else in your future? You divorce this individual and move on with your life, but can you really move on and leave the past behind?

You would have to be a very strong person to completely forget what happened in the past and give everyone 100 percent of your trust in the future. Even if you find a great person, and they seem to

be everything you have always wanted, how can you possibly forget
that the last person felt the same way to you too? The last person said
they loved you and swore they would never cheat on you, but they
did, so what is going to make this relationship any different? If your
new spouse comes home late from work, do you find yourself inter-
rogating them to find out where they have been and who they have
been with? Do you find yourself going through their wallet, phone
contacts, call records, credit card bills and car trying to find evidence
to support the story in your head, which is a result of the actions of
someone from your past? Is this new person going to be sentenced
to do the time, even though they did not commit the crime? Does
it make any sense to not trust anyone ever again because of the act
of only one person? Of course not, but that will be the temptation
unless you are willing to give up the story in your head.

Imagine a 12-year-old boy who loves basketball and plays as
much as he can. He joins a team to learn more about the sport and
get the expertise of a good coach. He enjoys the game a lot but is
struggling with confidence because sometimes when he misses a shot
in a game, the coach yells at him for taking the poor shot. Toward
the end of one game, the boy's team is down by just one point, and
there are only a few seconds left. The ball is passed to the young man
who takes the final shot in an effort to win the game for the team.
The ball bounces off the rim and fails to go in – much to everyone's
disappointment. He walks back to the bench where the team is in
a huddle focused on the coach. Instead of a pep talk and words of
encouragement, the coach turns to the young boy and says, *"How
does it feel to lose the game for the team?"*

Now imagine that the young man is 29 years old and working
for a large corporation in a management position. He attends many
high-level meetings where his input is needed, so the organization
can make strategic decisions. However, he is afraid to speak in these
meetings or offer his input, even though he has the expertise to offer.

His supervisor has even told him after the meetings and during reviews that he needs to start speaking up and offering his expertise.

Why is this young man afraid to speak up? It is simply because of the poorly chosen words and behaviors of a coach when he was 12 years old. In his mind, if he takes the shot and misses, there is a chance that he will get yelled at or told he lost the game for the team. The coach instilled the fear of failure into the boy, and now he carries it with him for the rest of his life. He is still hesitant to this day to take an emotional risk and offer his input (take the shot) because what if he does, and it is in contrast to other people's opinions, or he is wrong (the missed shot)? In his mind, if he never speaks up, he can never be wrong. If he never takes the shot, he can never miss. However, real life teaches us that you will never make the shot that you do not take. As easy as that is to quote, the act can be quite terrifying for you if you have an emotional wound from the past that the Gremlin holds up and reminds you of for the rest of your life.

real life teaches us that you will never make the shot that you do not take

At one of my seminars, I encountered an unusual circumstance that I found incredibly sad, but true. As part of the seminar, there is an exercise where I ask the attendees to write down the negative self-talk that is in their head. In other words, when they are considering taking some emotional risk and trying something new, pay attention to the words they hear in their head that try to talk them out of it. I ask everyone to write those disempowering words down, so they can develop an awareness of them. As part of the same exercise, I also ask them to write down their strengths or the truths about themselves. I have these same exercises in an earlier chapter of this book.

In this particular seminar, after the exercise was complete, I asked if anyone wanted to voluntarily share what they had written. A woman who was in her mid-40's raised her hand and began reading the negative self-talk that is in her head. I cannot remember the exact words because I was in such shock at the time, but here is my version of what I remember her saying:

- *You are stupid*
- *You are a loser*
- *No one likes you*
- *You have no future*
- *No one could ever love you*
- *You will never amount to anything*

The words above may not seem unusual for a Gremlin because your Gremlin can be heartless and cruel in the way it tries to control and dominate you with lies. But what made this story appalling beyond belief is that the woman said that it was her own grandmother who told her these things repeatedly when she was young. These words had been rolling around in her head since she was a little girl because her grandmother injected them into her.

I have no idea what could have been the motivation for a grandmother, or any relative, to poison a young mind and destroy a child's feeling of self-worth. The woman from the seminar is certainly aware that those things are not true, but she still hears the voice in her head, and it continues to influence her behaviors. If someone that is supposed to love and protect you feels this way about you, how could anyone else love you? If your own grandmother feels this way about you, then other people who are not as close to you must feel the same way too. Even though it may seem easy to rationalize that the grandmother is simply a nut case, and this woman should not pay any attention to what she said, it is easier said than done.

How much of an influence do people from your past have on your internal dialogue today? Look back into your past and think if you ever heard things like:

- *"Nothing in life comes easy"*

- *"Money is the root of all evil"*
- *"Money doesn't grow on trees"*
- *"Some people have all the luck"*
- *"You will never amount to anything"*
- *"The rich get richer and the poor get poorer"*
- *"If it wasn't for bad luck, I would have no luck at all"*

My encouragement to you is to be aware that these words or personal mantras are not yours – they are someone else's. These are the lenses by which someone else has viewed the world based on their own experiences, or ones that have been passed down to them. These are things that should not be inherited and passed down through the generations because they are not your experiences, they are someone else's. This is the way life was perceived for whoever developed the belief, and it may have become their internal script that painted their life as it is or as it was. It is up to you to write your own powerful script. It should be a script that screams personal power and should be void of victimization. Remember, no thought lives rent free in your head, so make sure the thoughts you leave in your head create a powerful and positive future without limitations. I would also encourage you to avoid ever leaving a victim in your wake by the words you use or your actions. Ask yourself this one question after your interaction with each person you encounter in life: "Are they better off now than before our interaction?" If you can have a positive influence on others, it will feed your soul, and you will have an extraordinary career and life and achieve your greatest desires.

Chapter 15

WE TAKE OURSELVES
WHEREVER WE GO

It is very rare to find someone who can have a specific set of thoughts and behaviors at work and be completely the opposite in their personal life. If you plan on making positive changes in your life, especially with respect to your thoughts and behaviors, you must make them a part of your entire life. The definition of holistic is *"including or involving all of something, especially all of somebody's physical, mental, and social conditions in change."* What this means is that if you plan on changing your behavior, you must make the changes in all areas of your life because it is very unlikely you will change behaviors at work and not at home (and vice versa). If change is going to occur, you must make the changes in all areas of your life (holistically = all encompassing). Here are just a few of the personality traits or behavior types that are commonplace in our society today:

- *Victim*
- *Pleaser*
- *Addictive*
- *Controller*
- *Disciplined*

- *Perfectionist*
- *Lack of Integrity*
- *Anger management problems*

If you have (or lack) any of these behaviors at work, there is a huge possibility that you are that way at home as well. This is a good example why I say that we take ourselves wherever we go. Let's look at each of the above and see how they might impact our lives.

Let's start with **victims**. The greatest thing about being a victim is it requires no action on your part. If you are a victim, you have convinced yourself that you have no choice and therefore there is nothing you can do to improve your situation. You are frozen in time and waiting for someone to rescue you. Everything that goes wrong in your life is someone else's fault. We all know people like this, and when they are at work, anything that goes wrong at work is someone else's fault, and they have excuses. Excuses are simply beliefs that if bought into, make you stuck in time and allow you to feel like a victim. Victims will rarely accept responsibility for their actions, and their finger is normally pointed at someone else when it comes to the blame game. After work, when they are far removed from work, they are not far removed from their thoughts, feelings and beliefs. If something goes wrong in their personal life, then once again, it is not their fault, and they are simply victims of someone else's actions. Victims need to get off cruise control, grab the steering wheel and take control of their own lives; it is the only answer to living an extraordinary life. You can go back to Chapter Five if you want to read more about victimization.

Pleasers have hearts of gold and all the best intentions. When they are at work, they hate to ask anyone to do too much, so they take on the larger share of the work because they don't want to inconvenience anyone else. They want people to like them (Gremlin issue), so they go out of their way to please everyone at the expense of themselves and their own health. People take pleasers for granted because they will take on more work than they should and never say "No," so they are easy to dump work on. When they get home at the end of a long work day, they continue their pleasing journey and fall prey to their families who also take them for granted. Pleasers will arrive home exhausted but still cook dinner, do the laundry, clean the house, mow the lawn and help the kids with their homework. At the end of the night, they have no time and energy left for anything or anyone, especially for themselves.

They are selfless in their actions both at work and in their personal lives, but I would encourage them to know their limits and learn to use the word "No." It does not make you a bad person if you use the word "No;" it simply lets everyone know your boundaries, which is a good thing. Pleasers also unknowingly disable others because they do everything for everybody, so the people around them never learn the tasks or duties that should be expected of them. In their effort to please others, they keep others from deeper learning and the feelings of gratification from doing a good job. They unknowingly rob people of their own self-worth and the satisfaction of a job well done. Pleasers need to understand that if they change their ways, people will still love and adore them. They need to stop listening to the Gremlin's threat that people are not going to like them, and instead, focus on how to best serve the people around them by letting people do things for themselves. The end result, if you are a pleaser, is that people will still love you, and in addition, they will respect you for making them feel valued.

People who have a **lack of integrity** in the workplace are just as likely to be corrupt in their personal lives as well. They might even try to justify why it is acceptable to steal money, office equipment or tools from work, or just as bad, steal time. They might say that they are underpaid for the work they do, and therefore the company owes them. They might try to convince you that their boss is a jerk, and they want to pay them back for the way they are treated, so they steal to punish him or her. People who try to justify why it is acceptable to steal are very much like victims because they believe someone else is to blame for their poor behaviors.

If I was married to someone who came home at the end of the day admitting to stealing from work, I would be hard-pressed to trust them in anything they do. If they can justify that stealing is acceptable because of something the boss or company did, then they might also try to justify that it is alright for them to cheat on me because of something I might do. I truly believe it is a door that once opened, is easy to walk through at your convenience. It will always be easy to find someone to blame for your actions because it protects you from feeling bad about your actions. Integrity has no scale of measure in my opinion because you either have it or you don't.

People with **addictive** personalities cannot separate their work world from their personal lives because addictions can completely engulf you. Whether it is smoking, drinking, drugs, sex, food, or any of the other lists of addictions that exist today, it is not easy to walk away from addictions at any point in your day or life. If you have the cravings at work, you are certainly going to have them in your personal life as well. If you are going to manage them, you will need professional assistance to help you gain control over all areas of your life. Addictions certainly require more action than simply learning to manage your Gremlin; they need professional care that can provide you with long term results that will serve you in all areas of your life. Unfortunately, addictions are not just about you because they have huge negative impacts on everyone in your business and personal life, so it is well worth the effort to seek solutions for them.

The next group of people are called **controllers,** and you know who you are. You are the most stressed of all the groups because you have undertaken a characteristic and behavior that is impossible to fulfill. My estimate from the years of doing seminars and coaching is that about 20 percent of the people I encounter in my leadership training are controllers. Out of that 20 percent, approximately half of them are controllers who also have compulsive behaviors. Let's talk for a moment about the challenges to being a controller.

First, no one wants to be controlled, so everyone around you is stressed because you are trying to control them, and they resent you for attempting to do so. Second, since you cannot control people because they do not want to be controlled, you have set yourself up for failure by attempting to do something that is impossible. To summarize: you are stressed because you are failing at trying to control people. On top of it, everyone around you at work and in your personal life is stressed because you are trying to control them, and they resent you for trying to do so.

Going back to the title of this chapter, "We Take Ourselves Wherever We Go," being a controller is another great example of how you will impact people at both work and home. You cannot control your impulse to control people and things, even though you know you cannot do it, and everyone around you resents you, or even worse, hates you for trying to do it. Control denotes "absolute power," which is a complete myth because it is unattainable. You have set yourself up for failure by accepting a task that is impossible, so give it up before you drive everyone out of your life. People who are controllers are normally that way because they feel out of control of their own lives. The basic fact is: if you are in control of your own emotions and your own life, you may not feel the need to control others. If you feel the need to control others at work or at home, take some time to analyze what part of your life is out of control, and then address those issues and stop trying to control other people.

People who are not **disciplined** in parts of their lives normally lack discipline in other areas of their lives as well. If you are overweight because you are not disciplined enough to eat right and exercise on a regular basis, then there are probably other areas of your life which show the same lack of discipline (I am not talking about people with medical challenges, I am talking about people with discipline challenges). If I was going to look for a great employee, I would go to the gym at 5 a.m. and look for the people who are there every single day working out at such an unreasonable hour because it shows a tremendous amount of discipline, which most people do not have. Once again, if someone is disciplined in their personal lives, you will more than likely find they are also very well disciplined at work.

If you are late for appointments or meetings at work on a regular basis, it is more than likely you are late when meeting friends and relatives for personal events as well. If you have a lack of consideration for other people's time in part of your life, you will more than likely lack it in other parts of your life as well. If you take shortcuts with your work projects and lack attention to detail, then my guess is that this occurs in other parts of your life as well. If you are lazy at work, you are more than likely lazy at home. This list goes on and on.

I have known people who show up late for appointments and do not return calls. They are the same ones who pay bills late and have their power or water turned off because they did not pay attention to the billing dates and warning notices they got in the mail. They cannot understand why their clients are unhappy and refuse to pay their bills when the work is not done in a timely manner. They, too, step into the victim mentality and blame their poor cash flow or lack of success on their "unreasonable" clients or other people in their personal or business lives that do not graciously accept their lack of discipline and failure to perform. If you are disciplined in part of your life, you will be disciplined in all areas of your life, and I always paid attention to that when I was interviewing potential employees.

Perfectionists are adorable because they believe their behavior or personality characteristic is a positive attribute. They have convinced themselves, and they will try to convince you, that their compulsive attention to detail is a great thing and helps make the world a better place to live in. The problem with perfectionists is that they sometimes move with such caution because they do not want to make any mistakes, and in the process of moving too slow, they become a barrier or bottleneck to success. Perfectionism is simply a fear disguised as a strength. One of the challenges with this state of mind is that perfection by humans is unattainable, so you are setting yourself up for an impossible task. You are setting your standards so high that you will beat yourself up if perfection is not attained.

As a matter of fact, perfectionists may also be prone to not wanting to try new things because they fear they may not be good enough. In other words, a perfectionist may try golf once, and if they are not good at it on the first try (which no one is), they will give it up because they weren't good enough. A child who is a perfectionist may play a video or board game with their friends, but if they are beat, they may not want to play again because they were not good enough. Perfectionists want to be perfect at everything or the tendency is to not participate because it is too emotionally traumatizing for them. As we have talked about earlier in the book, even though perfection is unattainable, excellence is attainable by humans, so that would be a more realistic and less stressful goal.

perfection by humans is unattainable

People who have **anger management problems** and exhibit their frustrations verbally (sometimes with robust body language) at work, normally have the same behaviors at home. If they are a yeller at work, then in most cases they are a yeller at home. If they blow up at their employees, co-workers, supervisor or customers at work, then they are more than likely doing the same thing to their significant other, children, family and friends at home. For many people, this is a learned behavior they saw their father or mother use to control and dominate the house with their loud voice and violent reactions.

I can honestly tell you that in my 35 or more years of leading people, you would be hard-pressed to find anyone who has ever heard me yell or scream at them. If you talk to my family and friends, they would have to search very hard to find the few times when I have raised my voice to any of them. It is not that I am not capable of the behavior, but I find very little value in using anger as a tool for anything. I just do not think it serves me or anyone in my presence very well, so I choose not to use it. My personal belief is that if I have to raise my voice to make a point, then I probably don't have a strong enough point to make on its own. If I am having a discussion with someone, and I feel the need to raise my voice to gain control of the conversation, then it means my talking points must be too weak, I am not well prepared or my point of view will not stand up on its own merit.

Yelling, in most cases, is about control and domination. If you feel you are losing control, you will raise your voice or exhibit aggressive behavior to try to regain control. For many people, yelling is fear being masked as something else, which is the fear of losing control. If you do not subscribe to my beliefs, then that is alright, just don't call and yell at me.

Yelling can certainly be more harmless, as in the case of fear masked as anger. If your child is playing near the street and runs into the road in front of an oncoming car, then you might yell at them, but that can simply be fear masquerading as anger. The anger management problem I am talking about is a behavior habit that the person chooses to not control, which leaves emotional wounds on other people. The worst part about this behavior is the end result, both at work and home, which is resentment from the people around you and the eventual physical or emotional retaliation. The habit can also become generational, and our children will learn it from us unless we stop the chain now and learn to control ourselves.

Regardless of which personality trait or behavior type you have adopted, the question for you is "Are you willing to change if change is needed?" Most of the previously described characteristics are not good for you and the people in your life, so is it important enough for you to want to change? If the goal is to live an extraordinary life and achieve your greatest desires, then will these behaviors impede on those goals? The Gremlin is not going to want you to change because it is afraid of the unknown, so it may try to convince you that change is not required. It may try to act as your ally and tell you that there is no need to change; you are fine just as you are, and other people are the problem, not you.

How often do you find yourself saying "No" to change? The word "No" requires very little action, and in most cases means you don't have to change anything. Do you remember Jim Carey's 2008 movie titled *Yes Man*? He played a character named Carl Allen who said "No" to everything and was at a standstill in his life, with no future in sight until the day he enrolls in a personal development program based on a very simple idea: say yes to everything. Carl discovers with amazement the magical power of "Yes," and sees both his professional and romantic life turned around overnight with an unexpected promotion and a new girlfriend.

What do you need to start saying "Yes" to instead of falling back into the auto-responder mode of "No," which requires no action on your part? Change is a choice, and not an easy one, because the Gremlin will want to keep you the way you are. However, remember, if you choose to want to change, practice these changes in both your personal and professional life because you cannot achieve it in one and not the other. We are simply incapable, in most cases, of having one behavior habit at work and a completely different behavior habit at home, so you must work at change in all areas of your life. Once change becomes holistic, you will unleash the power within you, and the extraordinary career and life that you have been seeking is one giant step closer.

Chapter 16

YOUR VALUES ARE NOT INVISIBLE

A s soon as you begin to speak, people you encounter begin to evaluate you by what you say, how you say it and what you look like as you speak. They are also evaluating your values by what you say, your behavior and your actions. Your values can be defined as the principles and standards by which you make decisions and how you live your life. They are the things that you value most in life, or in your business, and they are intangible. Intangible means your values cannot be seen or touched, but they are not invisible to the people around you.

Your values help define your character, and until the people you meet establish your character and connect with it, they will be very cautious about making too much of a commitment to you. Values are filters and guides for our personal life and can also guide our business as well because they influence our thoughts, feelings, words and actions. Your values are reflected in your goals, hopes, dreams, attitudes, interests, opinions, convictions, behaviors and actions, as well as your challenges in life. In your personal life, they influence your personality and give direction to your life. They can act as your internal compass and help keep you from going off course.

Tiger Wood's life went way off course, and it became a huge media event in 2010. It was discovered that he had been cheating on his wife with numerous women, and they all seemed to find some joy and financial gain in jumping into the media circus to tell their story. As they were making money from this horrible event, Tiger was losing millions of dollars in lost endorsement deals and sponsors wanting to distance themselves from his behaviors. He went from hero to villain overnight and lost the respect of millions of people around the world based on his behavior. His golf skills took a back seat to his human skills, which include his behavior.

Values are filters and guides for our personal life and can also guide our business as well

When he had his first news conference to talk about what he had done, one of the things he admitted to was that he had abandoned his core values, which included his religion. His moral compass was discarded, and it sent him in a direction that caused tremendous damage to himself, his wife, kids, family, friends, sponsors, the PGA and the entire golfing industry. His admitted selfish acts had a radial impact that he either failed to foresee or chose to ignore. This is the reason that it is important to define your core values and stay true to them.

If your values are the moral compass for your life and you have never taken the time to define your values, then how can the compass possibly work? How do you know where you are going, and how you are going to get there without it? I believe it is an exercise that anyone planning to get married should do. Each person should write their core values down separately and then compare them. They must be in harmony, or the relationship is more than likely doomed at some point. You must respect each other's values, or you will not be able to respect the other person. It would also be a good idea to have your teenagers take the time to define their core values as well, and your role is not to judge them for the values that they choose, but to help them stay true to their values. If you believe their values are questionable, then it would at least be an opportunity to have an open conversation about them to hear their story as to why those values are important to them.

One of my core values is integrity, and it is very important to me. If I found a wallet lying on a sidewalk with some type of identification in it, I would find a way to get it back to its owner. If there was no identification, I would contact the local police and turn the wallet over to them for safekeeping and hopeful return. The amount of money in the wallet would have nothing to do with my decision because the owner will get it back regardless. There is no amount of money that would motivate me to sell-out on my core values.

I actually lost my wallet in a movie theater recently. Once I got out of the theater and realized it had fallen out of my pocket, I immediately went back in and looked for it. It had only been about five minutes, but by the time I got back in there, it was gone. There had only been about eight people in the theater with us watching the movie, and they were all adults who looked just like us. The difference is, one of them made the decision that the contents of that wallet were more important to them than their own values. There were a couple of credit cards and $300 cash in the wallet, and evidently it was enough to motivate them to steal. I actually believe it is possible that this same person, if asked earlier in the day to write their core values down, could have written integrity or honesty. However, when challenged, there was a certain value or dollar amount at which they were willing to sell out on their values just like Tiger did. This is truly the determining factor as to whether it is a core value for you or not. Is there a certain dollar value that would motivate you to abandon your values? If so, it is not a core value.

In the business world, the first thing I do when facilitating strategic planning sessions is to help organizations define their top five core values. I do this because an organization also needs a compass to help them make decisions that serve them well. This compass helps them stay on track and creates a consistent message and focus for the organization. Everyone in the organization, from the CEO down to the front-line employees, is responsible for adhering to the core values of the organization. Five is not necessarily a magic number, and many times, we end up with four or six, if they are important enough to be taken into consideration.

Many times, organizations will define core values that they are not necessarily good at today, but they want to become better at. In other words, a few of my clients have asked me to perform employee satisfaction surveys in order to find out how the employees feel about the culture and leadership in the organization. The results showed that the employees thought communication and teamwork were poor and needed to be improved upon in order for them to enjoy their jobs more and for the organization to be more effective. So we revisited the core values of the organization and included communication and teamwork as two of their new core values in order to create more focus on these two issues. The new core values were also presented to all the employees, and they were notified that everyone was going to be held to a higher standard in these two areas. It put focus and intention on them, which created a behavior change in many employees.

In organizations, values are sometimes defined and then tucked neatly away into a policy manual to never be seen again. If you ask employees what the core values of their organization are, most would be hard pressed to come up with an answer. An organization's core values are useless unless promoted and discussed on a regular basis. The core values are the filter and compass that everyone should be passing their business decisions through, so if they do not know what is expected of them, how can they apply the filter?

I would encourage every organization to have their core values posted on their Web site, along with their mission statement and vision statement. The values should be on every job duty list for each employee, and they should be held to those values, just like all their other duties (and they should sign one copy for their records acknowledging that they will adhere to the duties and values). They should be listed on job applications, so people are aware, in advance, what kind of organization they are applying to, and if they cannot adhere to those values, then they should not apply. The values should be discussed on every employee evaluation, and each person should be evaluated or scored on how well they adhere to the organization's values. I would like you to apply this same kind of attention to the values in your personal life as well. If they are defined and adhered to, you can stay on course to a fabulous future.

Once defined, your core values do not have to be carved in stone for the rest of your life. As you grow older and your circumstances change, so can your values (and sometimes for the better). Hopefully you do not change too dramatically, where you abandon all your core beliefs at one time. But it is not unusual to have one or two change from time to time as your world changes. As you accumulate more wealth, maybe philanthropy, generosity or charity becomes more important to you. If you retire and have more time, volunteering or concern for others might play a larger role in your life. There can also be circumstances or events in our lives that reshape our values, like accidents, illness, cancer, or the death of a loved one that can make us rethink what is important to us and what we value most.

How well do you know you? List your top five personal core values (the things you value the most):

1. _____

2. _____

3. _____

4. _____

5. _____

Examples of Core Values

Acceptance	Excellence
Accomplishment	Fairness
Accuracy	Faith
Appreciation	Family
Authenticity	Fearlessness
Balance	Fitness
Bravery	Fun
Commitment	Generosity
Communication	Giving
Compassion	Gratitude
Concern for Others	Happiness
Courage	Harmony
Creativity	Honesty
Determination	Humility
Dignity	Humor
Diversity	Independence
Empathy	Integrity
Enthusiasm	Intimacy

Joy	Self-control
Kindness	Selflessness
Knowledge	Service
Love	Sincerity
Loyalty	Spirituality
Mindfulness	Spontaneity
Openness	Stewardship
Optimism	Teamwork
Passion	Thankfulness
Perseverance	Timeliness
Persistence	Trust
Playfulness	Truth
Reasonableness	Uniqueness
Relaxation	Vigor
Respect	Vision
Restraint	Willingness
Sacrifice	Wisdom
Security	Youthfulness

The reason I put the core value list on a separate page and did not give you advance notice, is that I wanted you to dig deep for your values and not choose from a shopping list. When you truly define your core values, it is because your heart told you what was "Most important" to you and what you valued most, not because a list told you. I only offer this list because many people, even with the best explanation, do not understand what values look like. These are simply a few words that might help you define your core values and bring you one step closer to having an extraordinary career and life – and achieving your greatest desires.

Chapter 17

IS IT TIME TO RE-BRAND
YOURSELF?

Whatis a brand? The dictionary defines "brand" as *a distinct type or making an indelible mark or impression on somebody or something.* An example of branding would be if someone told you that they were thirsty and wanted a soft drink that comes in a bright red can, you might think of Coca-Cola. If someone told you they wanted a small device that would fit into their pocket, hold thousands of songs and play music, the iPod might come to mind. If you wanted to order a book on-line, one of the Web sites that might come to mind is Amazon.com. If you wanted to put on a black leather outfit, buy a noisy motorcycle and hit the open road, Harley Davidson might pop into your head. These are all brands that are unique or have left their mark on us as of the printing of this book (which could easily change and also be different for each of us).

The wonderful thing about being a human being is that you have the option to change and re-brand yourself into who you truly want to be. You do not have to accept the Gremlin's version of who it has tried to force you into being; you can create your own brand and destiny. As we discussed earlier in this book, life is all about choices, rewards and consequences. The question to yourself is: do I live an extraordinary life and how well have I done at achieving my greatest desires? That is what this book is all about, and the question is not a fairy tale question with an impossible ending because you can achieve your desires if you choose to.

If you did not take the time to complete the exercises in this book, I would encourage you to go back and do so because the work is important if you plan on becoming who you want to be. You can be anything you want to be if you have a strong enough desire. There is nothing standing in your way except you and the thoughts rolling around in your head. If you follow the steps in this book, you can rewrite the script in your head, follow your moral compass with your core values, and begin managing

I truly believe that the biggest risks bring the biggest rewards

your own life instead of continuing to allow the Gremlin to manage you (which it is doing every single day).

If your desire is having the perfect love, a dream home, exotic car, world travel, early retirement, earning a master's degree, stopping smoking, losing weight, running a marathon, or simply living a stress-free life, it is attainable, and it has nothing to do with your I.Q., grade point, how lucky you are or how much money you have today. These things, and more, are attainable if you believe they are, and if you do things to build your confidence, plus learn how to manage your fears. I truly believe that the biggest risks bring the biggest rewards, but risk involves fear. As you have learned from this book, fear is simply the anticipation of pain. Anytime you choose to go after one of your desires, the Gremlin will try to scare you back to conformity by threatening you with the possibility of failure, rejection, humiliation or embarrassment. One of the biggest lessons to learn about the Gremlin is that it lies and its threats are, for the most part, fables that will never come true. So if most of the things we fear or worry about never come true, then why on earth do we listen to the Gremlin? Because it masks itself as our friend and ally, and we believe it is trying to help us and protect us from pain.

Re-branding yourself into a more powerful you may require a new script that is authentically you. It may require you to get rid of your current script, which is the one that the Gremlin wrote for you (and we know that this little bugger lies, lies, lies). Your new brand should make you distinct and allow you to make an indelible mark or impression on the world. Your new brand should not be fake or made up words on a piece of paper that you are trying to convince yourself are real; it should be a script that you truly believe in. I am not a subscriber to the philosophy "Fake it until you make it."

In order to put some of what you have learned into action, please take a moment to write down on the Personal Action Plan below at least three things you will start doing differently, which will help you live an extraordinary life and achieve your greatest desires. Also write down three things that you need to stop doing in order to help you achieve your goals. Then write down at least three things that you already do, that help you have an extraordinary career and life, and achieve your greatest desires.

PERSONAL ACTION PLAN

I Will Start: _____

_____

_____

_____

I Will Stop: _____

_____

_____

_____

I Will Keep: _____

_____

_____

_____

SUMMARY

Up until about 2002, I am not sure I would have believed that I would be able to live an extraordinary life and achieve my greatest desires. I did live a great life up until then, so nothing felt broken. However, looking back, I let my Gremlin put limits on me. Over my lifetime, I was capable of so much more, but I let the Gremlin's voice hold me back and keep me from truly believing in myself. No one knew I had self-doubt because I have always carried myself with confidence, but it was a mask for what was truly underneath. I wish I would have known the things in this book when I was 18 years old because it would have made a huge difference in my life. The end result is fine because I do live a life that most people would envy, but I battled my Gremlin all the way to get here. Nothing came easy, and I had to work incredibly hard to get where I am today. I never discovered my Gremlin until I was 46 years old, so my goal, through this book and my seminars, is to access as many people as I can and educate them in their teens, 20s, 30s, or whatever age they are (heck, why not in their 70s or 80s too?), about the greatness that lies within them because I truly believe it's there in everyone. There are no age limits to being able to discover your Gremlin, live an extraordinary life or achieve your greatest desires. Is it your time? Are you ready?

Every person has unlimited potential to be and do whatever they choose if they simply believe in themselves. Success is just around the corner for so many people if they can apply what they have learned in this book. Success is different for everybody because for some it is about building wealth and for others it is about building a great relationship, serving the world or being stress-free and happy. None of these desires is wrong, and none should be judged because we are all on a different journey. It is important to enjoy the journey each day, through the good times and bad because I have learned that the destination is not as important as the joy of the journey.

I just hope that whatever your desires are, at the end of your journey, you look back and realize that you left nothing on the table, and you gave it your all. You have no regrets because you were authentic in your life and lived by your core values. You left no victims in your wake and everyone in your life is better off for knowing you. You achieved the desires that were "Most important" to you and have no regrets about the things you did not achieve. When you heard your Gremlin try to talk you down or whisper disempowering language in your ear in an effort to scare you into conformity, you recognized it, laughed at its lies and moved on with enthusiasm. You abandoned the Gremlin's script of who it wanted you to be, in place of the new, more powerful and true script about who you truly are.

You surround yourself with friends who are supportive of the true you and give you energy to keep up the journey of life. You set S.M.A.R.T. goals for yourself and never let fear stand in your way or thwart your efforts. When you set powerful new goals for yourself and when you get nervous about your commitment, you laugh and embrace the anxiety because you know that it is the Gremlin who is scared, not you. The butterflies in your stomach are from excitement, not fear, because you are living the life you have always dreamed of.

You make your life more intentional by methodically mapping and planning your goals in order to bring them to reality. If you did not achieve your goals on the first round, you did not bow your head in defeat; you readjusted and tried again until you were successful. You did not let the Gremlin's disempowering words like *"But what if..."* scare you and drive you back to the safety of inaction. You wake each day and choose a great attitude because it serves you and everyone around you well. Most importantly, you take time to celebrate the small victories and recognize yourself for your achievements.

Steps to an Extraordinary Career & Life:

1. *Make your desires "<u>Most</u> important" to you*
2. *Learn to manage your fears*
3. *Develop awareness of your Gremlin's voice*
4. *Read your new internal script daily*
5. *Associate with Energy Givers who support you*
6. *Set S.M.A.R.T. goals for yourself*
7. *"Idea Map" your goals so you have a plan*
8. *Be aware of disempowering language*
9. *Choose a great attitude*
10. *Celebrate your success*

Now that you have the steps to have an extraordinary career and life, and achieve your greatest desires, begin to live it, believe it and enjoy it. I truly believe that each of us has the capacity for greatness and that we can impact the world in tremendous ways if we choose. This book is just one more desire I have achieved because I learned to manage my Gremlin. By reading this book, you have made another of my desires become a reality, and I thank you for that.

**"No one can make us feel inferior without our permission" –
Eleanor Roosevelt**

ABOUT THE AUTHOR

Brad Worthley is the founder of Brad Worthley International, Inc., a Bellevue, Washington based consulting, coaching and training firm. An accomplished consultant with over 35 years of business management experience, he is also an internationally acclaimed leadership, customer service and motivational expert. He has trained hundreds of thousands of people throughout a wide range of industries. A true professional, Brad equips companies with dynamic customer service and leadership essentials. He teaches leading corporations how to consistently build and retain customer loyalty using his proven methods.

Brad is also the creator of a revolutionary new concept in modifying behavior called "Perception Awareness Training." This method keeps seminar participants entertained while helping them retain the information they learn. He is a master storyteller and delivers his powerful message from the customer's perspective with sincerity and humor. Many have referred to his lively presentations as "shows." Brad is always one of the highest rated speakers at any event he speaks at, and the common response from attendees is: *"When will he be back!"*

After college and an Associate of Science degree, Brad started his business career at the age of 20 by opening a sporting goods store. Since then, he has created and sold six other successful businesses in the fields of retail, wholesale, marketing, distribution and consulting. He has experienced every aspect of the business world, and not only talks the talk, but walks the walk.

Brad Worthley International produces training DVD's on customer service and leadership which are being used by organizations from all industries and all sizes throughout the world, as well as many audio programs and books. Brad writes two monthly electronic newsletters called "Insights and Strategies" which have thousands of loyal subscribers in over 75 countries (you can subscribe at www. BradWorthley.com).

Brad is a past President (2002/2003) of the Mystery Shopping Providers Association, whose goal is dedicated to improving customer service. He received the "Volunteer of the Year Award" for 2001, and in 2001, was honored with the "Hall of Fame" award, the highest honor in the industry.

Brad and Melanie have four fabulous children who share their extraordinary life and continue to help them achieve their greatest desires. In his spare time, Brad was a volunteer coach of youth sports for over 15 years (soccer, baseball and basketball). Brad also volunteers weekly with a local domestic violence organization where he works with children of victims.

For more information on his services, product, articles and resources, visit Brad Worthley on-line at www.BradWorthley.com, join Brad on www.Facebook.com/BradWorthley or follow him at www.Twitter.com/BradWorthley.

Brad Worthley International Services

Motivation Training Seminars:
- Simple Steps to an Extraordinary Career & Life

Customer Service Training Seminars:
- Exceeding Customer Expectations

Leadership Development Training Seminars:
- Turning Managers into Leaders
- How to Coach Your Employees, Peers & Supervisor
- Increase Communication & Increase Success
- Reduce Stress & Increase Productivity
- Different Generations, Different Challenges....Dude

Leadership Development Assessments

Personal Coaching:
- Owner/Manager Business Coaching
- Group Leadership Development Coaching
- Individual Leadership Development Coaching

Pre-Employment Testing for:
- Customer Service Positions
- Sales Positions
- Leadership Positions

Employee Surveys

Customer Surveys

Facilitation for Strategic Planning and Conflict Resolution

Keynote Speaker

For information on any of the above services, call (425)957-9696 in Bellevue, Washington or Email Brad@BradWorthley.com